weekend baking

weekend baking

easy recipes for relaxed family baking

RYLAND
PETERS
& SMALL

LONDON NEW YORK

Sarah Randell

photography by Kate Whitaker

Dedication
For my parents, for teaching me what good food is all about.

Design, Photographic Art Direction and Prop Styling Steve Painter
Senior Editor Céline Hughes
Production Controller Toby Marshall
Art Director Leslie Harrington
Publishing Director Alison Starling

Food Stylist Joss Herd
Food Stylist's Assistants Tim Jenner and Laura Fyfe
Indexer Hilary Bird

First published in the UK in 2010
by Ryland Peters & Small
20–21 Jockey's Fields
London WC1R 4BW
www.rylandpeters.com

10 9 8 7 6 5 4 3 2 1

Text © Sarah Randell 2010
Design and photographs
© Ryland Peters & Small 2010

Printed in China

ISBN: 978 1 84975 032 5

A CIP record for this book is available from the British Library.

Author's acknowledgements
Thank you to the team at Ryland Peters & Small, plus Kate Whitaker and the lovely Joss for such gorgeous pics.

And, a special thank you to B, for tasting umpteen cakes with me, both the successes and the slightly doubtful, with unfaltering enthusiasm and always, with a smile, x.

Publisher's acknowledgements
For kind loan of props:

Jane Wicks
Kitchenalia at 'Country Ways'
Strand Quay, Rye, East Sussex
Tel: 01797 227 210

Soendergaard Design for hand-thrown porcelain.
soendergaarddesign.co.uk

Kitchenaid for the loan of the electric stand mixer featured in this book. Visit www.kitchenaid.com for more of their products and your nearest stockist.

The lovely Kitty for being the perfect child model.

Nuala McArdle for hair and make-up.

Steve Painter and Nuala McArdle for allowing us to use their home in Hastings for location photography.

Notes
- All spoon measurements are based on measuring spoons and are level unless otherwise stated.
- Butter is salted, unless otherwise stated. If you need softened butter for a recipe, leave it at room temperature for several hours before you start. I leave it out of the fridge overnight if I am using it for baking the next day.
- All baking tin measurements given are base measurements. Use non-stick bakeware to avoid sticky moments.
- If you bake frequently, it is worth investing in reusable plastic baking liners to save on baking parchment.
- All eggs are large, unless otherwise stated. If possible, use eggs at room temperature.
- I like to use unrefined sugar, such as Billington's. (Visit www.billingtons.co.uk for their products.) The flavours are more complex than refined sugars and enhance the final results. A word of warning though – unrefined icing sugar isn't white, so although it can look gorgeous on some cakes, it may not always be the best option to use for icings and frostings!
- Ovens should be preheated to the specified temperature. Recipes in this book were tested using a regular oven. If using a fan-assisted oven, follow the manufacturer's instructions for adjusting temperatures.

contents

Introduction

A day spent in the kitchen, mixing and baking, with the radio murmuring in the background is, to me, a day well spent. The warmth of the oven and the deliciously sweet, spicy, chocolatey or citrussy smells that may waft from its tightly closed door are not only truly comforting but ultimately satisfying too. Whether it be a batch of buttery madeleines, a tray of fruit-packed muffins, some giant chocolate chip cookies or a traditional Victoria sandwich for a birthday cake, I guarantee you will feel wonderfully smug and proud as they cool on a rack in the kitchen, waiting to be devoured or coated in a whipped icing or sticky glaze.

Children tend to be particularly enthusiastic about helping when it comes to baking. There are plenty of opportunities for little fingers to taste from the bowl, helping to mix and then to decorate and show what they have made. I'm not suggesting that children should eat cake every day, nor that we adults should, but quiet interludes in the kitchen can be just as absorbing for them as for us and highly rewarding. The time it takes to bake a cake is, in my experience, as enjoyable as eating it.

If you are a beginner, there are lots of simple baking recipes here to tempt you. All you need is some time and a few basic tools. If you are buying new tins, I urge you to invest in some good-quality kit – it really will be worth it in the long run and will last for years. As for mixing, I have an electric mixer, which I use for nearly all my baking, but I used to rely on an electric hand whisk that I have now had for 20 years and it is still going strong. If you don't have anything similar, a mixing bowl and a balloon whisk or wooden spoon, accompanied by a bit of elbow grease, will usually suffice.

For more experienced cooks, there are some new ideas here to try and have fun with. Whatever takes your fancy, I hope sugar and spice become as big a part of your storecupboard in the future as they are mine. Happy baking.

small cakes

scones with strawberry jam and plenty of clotted cream

Scones are best eaten the day they are made, but they do freeze well if you have a few left over. Another time, try adding the grated zest of a lemon and a small handful of sultanas or chopped, stoned dates to the mix.

1 large egg

about 125 ml milk

a squeeze of lemon juice

225 g plain flour

2 rounded teaspoons baking powder

2 tablespoons caster sugar, plus extra for sprinkling

a pinch of salt

50 g butter, softened and cubed

strawberry jam, to serve

clotted cream, to serve

a plain 4–5-cm cookie cutter

a baking tray, oiled

Makes about 10

Preheat the oven to 220°C (425°F) Gas 7.

Put the egg and milk in a small jug and lightly beat, then mix in the lemon juice.

Sift the flour and baking powder into a large mixing bowl and stir in the 2 tablespoons of sugar and the salt.

Scatter the cubes of butter over the flour mixture and, using a table knife, cut them into the flour. Now, lightly rub the butter into the flour, using your fingertips, until the mixture resembles breadcrumbs.

Pour in half the egg mixture and, using the knife again, mix the liquid into the dry ingredients using a cutting action. Add as much of the remaining egg mixture as you need to, to be able to bring everything together into a dough – you probably won't need it all.

Tip the dough out onto a lightly floured work surface and gently pat it out until it is about 2.5 cm thick. Using the cutter, stamp out scones, then gently re-form the dough and continue until you have used it all.

Arrange the scones on the baking tray. Brush the tops with any leftover egg mixture and sprinkle generously with caster sugar. Bake in the preheated oven for 10–12 minutes, or until risen and golden.

Leave the scones to cool on a wire rack. Serve with generous amounts of jam and clotted cream to spread on the halved scones.

toffee pear muffins

The toffee in these muffins is dulce de leche: thick, luscious Argentinian caramel, sold in tins or jars. It also makes a delicious sauce to serve with sautéed pears, apples or bananas, for a quick pudding, if you have some left over.

150 g butter

150 ml milk

3 large eggs

6 tablespoons dulce de leche

100 g light brown soft sugar, plus extra for sprinkling

300 g self-raising flour

1 heaped teaspoon baking powder

2 rounded teaspoons mixed spice

2 large, ripe but firm pears, cored, peeled and chopped into small pieces

1 rounded tablespoon porridge oats

a 12-hole muffin tin, lined with paper muffin cases

Makes 12

Preheat the oven to 200°C (400°F) Gas 6

Melt the butter in a small pan and leave to cool slightly.

In a large mixing bowl and using a balloon whisk, whisk together the milk, eggs, 2 tablespoons of the dulce de leche, the 100 g of sugar and the melted butter.

Sift in the flour, baking powder and mixed spice and whisk together. Scatter the chopped pear over the top and, using a large metal spoon, gently fold it in until just combined.

Divide the mixture (which will be quite sloppy) between the muffin cases. Sprinkle each muffin with a little extra sugar and a few porridge oats. Bake the muffins in the preheated oven for 30–35 minutes, or until risen and lightly golden.

Leave the muffins to cool for 10 minutes or so, then, using a small, sharp knife, cut a small cross in the top of each muffin and spoon half a teaspoonful of dulce de leche into each one. Leave it to settle, then add another half a teaspoonful to sit on top. Eat while still warm.

chocolate heaven muffins

These muffins are bursting with chocolate and are as easy as pie to rustle up. For the ultimate chocolate experience, eat them fresh from the oven.

75 g butter

75 g dark chocolate (about 50% cocoa solids)

75 g milk chocolate

50 g white chocolate

100 g soured cream

50 ml milk

50 g light muscovado or light brown soft sugar

2 large eggs

175 g plain flour

2 tablespoons cocoa powder

1 tablespoon baking powder

a pinch of salt

1 tablespoon Demerara sugar

a 6-hole muffin tin, lined with paper muffin cases

Makes 6

Preheat the oven to 200°C (400°F) Gas 6.

Melt the butter in a small pan and leave to cool slightly.

Chop the three types of chocolate into small chunks.

In a large mixing bowl and using a balloon whisk, whisk together the soured cream, milk, muscovado sugar, eggs and melted butter.

Sift in the flour, cocoa and baking powder. Sprinkle in the salt and add all the chopped chocolate. Using a large metal spoon, fold everything together until combined, but don't over-mix.

Divide the mixture between the muffin cases. Sprinkle each muffin with a little Demerara sugar. Bake the muffins in the preheated oven for 20 minutes – by which time they will be risen, but still very slightly unset in the middle. They will continue to cook as they cool.

crunchy-topped raspberry and banana muffins

Delicious warm or cold, for breakfast or tea, these muffins are also ideal for packed lunches and they freeze well. Another time, use blueberries instead of the raspberries to ring the changes.

150 g butter

2 very ripe bananas

150 ml milk

150 g caster sugar

3 large eggs

300 g self-raising flour

1 slightly rounded teaspoon baking powder

150 g raspberries

3–4 tablespoons Demerara sugar

2 tablespoons sunflower seeds

a 12-hole muffin tin, lined with paper muffin cases

Makes 12

Preheat the oven to 200°C (400°F) Gas 6.

Melt the butter in a small pan and leave to cool slightly.

Peel and mash the bananas.

In a large mixing bowl and using a balloon whisk, whisk together the milk, caster sugar, eggs and melted butter.

Sift in the flour and baking powder and add the raspberries and banana. Using a large metal spoon, fold everything together until combined, but don't over-mix.

Divide the mixture between the muffin cases. Sprinkle each muffin with a little Demerara sugar and the sunflower seeds. Bake the muffins for 30–35 minutes, or until risen and golden. Leave to cool on a wire rack.

blueberry lime friands

If you haven't come across friands before, you will soon be converted. Based on the French *financier*, they are small, light-textured cakes and very moreish. If you don't want to invest in a special friand tin, you can make these in a regular muffin tin.

125 g butter

75 g shelled, blanched whole hazelnuts

125 g icing sugar

100 g plain flour

finely grated zest of 2 limes

175 g blueberries

4 large egg whites

Lime syrup

freshly squeezed juice of 1 small lime

40 g caster sugar

a 9-hole friand tin, well buttered

Makes 9

Preheat the oven to 200°C (400°F) Gas 6.

Melt the butter in a small pan and leave to cool slightly.

Whiz the hazelnuts in a blender until finely ground.

Sift the icing sugar and flour into a large mixing bowl. Stir in the ground hazelnuts, lime zest and blueberries.

Put the egg whites in a large, scrupulously clean bowl and whisk until they form soft peaks.

Using a large metal spoon, fold half the egg whites into the flour mixture with half the melted butter – be as gentle as you can be. Fold in the other half of the egg whites and melted butter.

Divide the mixture between the holes of the prepared friand tin. Bake in the preheated oven for 20 minutes.

To make the lime syrup, heat the lime juice and sugar together in a small pan, stirring, until all the sugar has dissolved.

Leave the cooked friands to cool for 5 minutes, then make a few holes in the top of each one using the point of a small, sharp knife. Carefully drizzle a little of the lime syrup over each of the warm cakes, allowing it to seep into the holes. Leave the friands in the tin until completely cold, before running a knife around the edges and turning them out.

vanilla cupcakes with raspberry frosting

These cakes, with their pretty pink frosting, are ideal for little girls' birthday parties and a good recipe to make with children. If you want to turn these into grown-up cakes, use the same frosting, but top each one with a fresh raspberry.

175 g butter, softened and cubed

175 g caster sugar

3 large eggs

175 g self-raising flour, sifted

3 tablespoons milk

1 teaspoon vanilla extract

tiny sugar balls, sprinkles or pink edible glitter, to decorate

Raspberry frosting

75 g unsalted butter

60 g raspberries

75 g caster sugar

150 g cream cheese, chilled

a 12-hole muffin tin, lined with paper cupcake cases

Makes 10

Preheat the oven to 180°C (350°F) Gas 4.

Put the butter, sugar, eggs and flour in an electric mixer (or use a large mixing bowl and an electric whisk). Whisk together for a few minutes to combine. Add the milk and vanilla extract and whisk again.

Divide the mixture between the cupcake cases. Bake in the preheated oven for 25–30 minutes, or until risen and golden. Leave to cool on a wire rack.

To make the raspberry frosting, melt the butter in a small pan and leave to cool slightly.

Put the raspberries in a separate small pan and heat up – just until they reach simmering point and become a seedy purée. Take the pan off the heat and tip the purée into a coarse sieve set over a small bowl. Sieve the purée, leave the juice to cool and discard the seeds.

Whisk together the sugar and cream cheese. Add the melted butter and whisk again. Finally, add 2 teaspoons of the cooled raspberry juice and mix again. You are aiming for a pretty pink colour, so add more juice as necessary. Chill the frosting until the cupcakes have completely cooled.

Top each cake with pink frosting – you can spread it on with a spatula, or use a piping bag, as you wish. Decorate with sugar balls, sprinkles or edible glitter.

ginger meringues

Meringues really are easy to make and, if you want to get ahead, they will keep for a couple of days in an airtight tin before sandwiching together.

3 large egg whites

185 g caster sugar

1 ball stem ginger in syrup, drained and very finely chopped

Ginger cream

150 ml double cream

1 ball stem ginger in syrup, drained and very finely chopped

2 baking trays, lined with baking parchment (don't grease it, or your egg whites will collapse!)

Makes 15

Preheat the oven to 140°C (275°F) Gas 1.

Put the egg whites in a large, scrupulously clean bowl and whisk until they form stiff peaks. Now, gradually add the sugar – in tablespoonfuls – whisking all the time. You will end up with a smooth, thick, glossy meringue. Using a large metal spoon, gently fold in the chopped ginger.

Using a teaspoon, make 15 small mounds on each of the prepared baking trays, swirling each mound into a peak using the end of a skewer. Each meringue should be 4–5 cm in diameter at the base.

Bake in the preheated oven for 30 minutes, then turn off the oven and leave the meringues in it until completely cold, ideally overnight.

To make the ginger cream, whip the cream until it forms soft peaks, then stir in the chopped ginger. Use to sandwich the meringues together in pairs.

mini chocolate, beetroot and cherry cakes

Using beetroot in these cakes gives them slightly squidgy centres and they freeze well, before decorating. If you are making them as a gift, dust the tops with cocoa, then sprinkle with edible mini gold balls – dip the end of your finger in a little cold water before applying so that they stick.

75 g dark chocolate
(about 50% cocoa solids)

50 g dried sour cherries
(or dried cranberries)

175 g self-raising flour

40 g cocoa powder

175 g light muscovado or
light brown soft sugar

250 ml groundnut or
vegetable oil

3 large eggs

a pinch of salt

150 g cooked, peeled
beetroot

a 9-hole petite loaf tin (base measurement of each hole 5.5 x 8 cm and 2.5 cm deep), lined with paper mini-loaf cases

Makes 9

Preheat the oven to 180°C (350°F) Gas 4.

Break the chocolate into pieces and melt it in a heatproof bowl set over a pan of barely simmering water. Leave to cool slightly.

Roughly chop the sour cherries.

Sift the flour into an electric mixer (or use a large mixing bowl and an electric whisk). Add the cocoa, sugar, oil, eggs, salt and the melted chocolate, and whisk until combined. Using the coarse side of a grater, grate the beetroot into the mixture and sprinkle in the chopped sour cherries. Using a large metal spoon, fold everything together gently.

Divide the mixture between the loaf cases. Bake in the preheated oven for 20–25 minutes, or until well risen. Leave the cakes to cool completely in the tin.

Note: The petite loaf tin and matching cases needed for these cakes can be bought from www.janeasher.co.uk. If you prefer, you can bake the cakes in muffin cases instead of mini-loaf cases – they will take 25–30 minutes in the oven, and make 9 muffins.

honey and rosemary madeleines

I like to use eucalyptus or Greek honey to make these, as it partners well with the delicate flavour of the rosemary, but you can, of course, use any runny honey. If you want to keep things really simple, they are equally delicious without the rosemary. Madeleines are best eaten fresh on the day of baking, but they do freeze well.

75 g butter

2 tablespoons runny honey

2 fresh rosemary sprigs

2 large eggs

100 g caster sugar

50 g self-raising flour

½ teaspoon baking powder

50 g ground almonds

a small pinch of salt

a 12-hole madeleine tin, well buttered and lightly dusted with flour

Makes 18

Put the butter, honey and sprigs of rosemary in a small pan over the lowest possible heat. Heat gently, giving it a swirl now and then. Take the pan off the heat and leave the mixture to cool and infuse for 15 minutes.

Put the eggs and sugar in an electric mixer (or use a large mixing bowl and an electric whisk) and whisk until pale and mousse-like – this can take up to 10 minutes.

Preheat the oven to 200°C (400°F) Gas 6.

Sift the flour into a large mixing bowl and stir in the baking powder, almonds and salt. Add half the melted butter mixture (removing the sprigs of rosemary as you do so) and half the flour mixture to the beaten eggs and sugar. Using a large metal spoon, fold everything together quickly but gently. Repeat this process with the remaining melted butter mixture and the flour mixture.

Fill the holes of the madeleine tin with mixture. Bake the madeleines in the preheated oven for 8–10 minutes, or until golden and risen. Leave the madeleines to cool in the tin for a couple of minutes, then remove (you may need a table knife to help ease them out) and transfer to a wire rack. Wash, re-grease and re-flour the tin before baking the remaining mixture. You should make 18 madeleines in total.

plum, orange and double almond crumble tartlets

If you are not a confident pastry maker, you shouldn't have any problems here, as this is a well-behaved pastry recipe. These tartlets can also be turned into mince pies for Christmas – just substitute the jam and plums with 400 g mincemeat.

Pastry base

200 g plain flour

100 g unsalted butter, softened

1 tablespoon icing sugar, plus extra for dusting (optional)

1 large egg, lightly beaten

Crumble filling

75 g Demerara sugar

25 g unsalted butter, chilled and cubed

50 g plain flour

25 g rolled oats

1 heaped tablespoon flaked almonds

grated zest of 1 large orange (use a zester, if you have one, rather than a fine grater)

3 ripe but firm plums

25 g shelled almonds (skin on)

7–8 tablespoons plum jam, such as Victoria or damson

a fluted 9-cm cookie cutter

2 x 12-hole muffin tins, oiled

Makes 24

To make the pastry base, put the flour, butter and icing sugar in an electric mixer. Mix for a minute or until the mixture resembles breadcrumbs. Add the egg and briefly mix again. As soon as the pastry starts to come together, tip it onto the work surface and bring it together in a ball. Press the ball into a disc, wrap in clingfilm and chill it for 30 minutes.

To make the crumble filling, briefly mix the sugar, butter and flour in the electric mixer, again until the mixture resembles breadcrumbs. Stir in the oats, flaked almonds and orange zest.

On a lightly floured work surface, roll out the pastry until it is about 2 mm thick. It may be easier to roll out half at a time. Using the cutter, stamp out rounds and use to line the holes of the tins – the pastry will come about halfway up the side of each hole. Gently re-form and re-roll the pastry, then keep stamping out rounds until you have 24. Chill the pastry-lined tins for 30 minutes.

Meanwhile, halve, stone and chop the plums into pea-sized pieces. Roughly chop the whole almonds.

Preheat the oven to 200°C (400°F) Gas 6.

Put a teaspoon of jam in each pastry case, then divide the chopped plum between them, followed by the crumble. Sprinkle each with chopped almonds.

Bake the tartlets in the preheated oven for 15–18 minutes, or until golden. Leave to cool for 5 minutes, then transfer to a wire rack. Eat warm or cold but not hot, as the jam will burn easily. Dust with icing sugar, if you like.

coffee and pecan cupcakes with praline

These are best made and eaten on the same day, but the undecorated cakes will keep well in the freezer if you want to make a batch to decorate later. If time is really short, top them with a simple coffee-flavoured water icing instead of the frosting and praline.

3 tablespoons instant coffee granules

6 tablespoons boiling water

275 g caster sugar, plus 2 tablespoons

175 g butter, softened and cubed

3 large eggs

175 g self-raising flour

100 g pecan halves, chopped

Frosting

200 g icing sugar

2 tablespoons crème fraîche

150 g unsalted butter, softened

2 x 12-hole muffin tins, lined with paper cupcake cases

a baking tray, lined with baking parchment

Makes 15

Preheat the oven to 180°C (350°F) Gas 4.

Tip the coffee into a cup with the boiling water and the 2 tablespoons of caster sugar. Stir together for a minute or so until the sugar has dissolved. Leave to cool.

Put the butter, 175 g of the caster sugar and the eggs in the bowl of an electric mixer (or use a large mixing bowl and an electric whisk). Sift in the flour, drizzle in 3 tablespoons of the coffee syrup and whisk together for a few minutes to combine. Stir half the pecans into the mixture; reserve the other half for the praline.

Divide the mixture between the cupcake cases. Bake in the preheated oven for 20 minutes, or until risen and lightly golden. Transfer the cupcakes to a wire rack. While they are still warm, make a few fork indentations in the top of each one and carefully drizzle over a little of the remaining coffee syrup, letting it seep into the cakes as you do so. Leave to cool completely.

Next, make the praline. Tip the remaining 100 g caster sugar into a medium pan or frying pan over low heat and heat gently. As soon as it has melted, increase the heat a little and let the sugar simmer and gradually turn to a deep golden caramel. Tip in the reserved pecans, give everything a quick stir and tip the hot praline onto the prepared baking tray. Spread it out slightly, then leave until cold and set.

To make the frosting, sift the icing sugar into a bowl, add the crème fraîche and the butter and beat together until smooth.

Spread the frosting onto the cold cupcakes with a round-bladed knife. Bash the praline with the end of a rolling pin to break it up, then crumble some on top of each cake.

spiced pumpkin cheesecakes with nutmeg icing

Have fun with these for Halloween – use themed cupcake cases and decorate with sugarcraft sprinkles.

Cheesecakes

75 g butter

125 g shortcake or shortbread biscuits, broken into pieces

200 g cream cheese

100 g soft curd cheese

100 g tinned pumpkin purée

100 g caster sugar

2 medium eggs, lightly beaten

2 pinches each of ground cloves, ginger, allspice and nutmeg

orange sanding sugar, to decorate (optional)

Nutmeg icing

50 g caster sugar

100 g cream cheese

½ teaspoon freshly grated nutmeg

a 12-hole muffin tin, lined with paper cupcake cases

Makes 12

Preheat the oven to 150°C (300°F) Gas 3.

First make the biscuit base for the cheesecakes. Melt the butter in a small pan and leave to cool slightly.

Grind the biscuits to crumbs in a food processor. Add all but 1 tablespoon of the melted butter (reserve this for the icing) and whiz to combine. Divide between the cupcake cases and press down firmly with the back of a teaspoon.

Put the cream cheese, curd cheese, pumpkin purée, sugar, beaten eggs and spices in an electric mixer (or use a large mixing bowl and an electric whisk). Whisk until smooth and combined. Tip the mixture into a jug, then pour it into the cupcake cases, dividing it equally.

Bake the cakes in the preheated oven for 15 minutes. Leave to cool completely – they will set as they cool.

To make the nutmeg icing, whisk the ingredients together (including the reserved butter) and put a spoonful on each cheesecake. If you are not eating them immediately, refrigerate them but let them come to room temperature before eating. Sprinkle with sanding sugar, if you like. They are soft-set, so they are best eaten with teaspoons.

cookies & biscuits

prune, cinnamon and toasted walnut cookies with cinnamon icing

Agen prunes are a juicy and delicious addition to these chewy cookies, but raisins would also be a good choice. If you are making the cookies at Christmastime or are feeling decadent, substitute half the water in the icing with Armagnac.

75 g walnut pieces

100 g butter, softened

150 g light brown soft sugar

1 large egg, lightly beaten

2 tablespoons cream cheese

75 g light brown and
75 g white self-raising flour
(or use all white flour)

2 teaspoons ground
cinnamon

a pinch of salt

125 g stoned, soft Agen
prunes, snipped into small
pieces

Cinnamon icing

50 g icing sugar

2 or 3 pinches of ground
cinnamon

2 baking trays, oiled

Makes about 20

Preheat the oven to 200°C (400°F) Gas 6.

Spread the walnuts on a baking tray and toast in the preheated oven for 5 minutes, then leave to cool.

Put the butter and sugar in an electric mixer (or use a large mixing bowl and an electric whisk) and beat until light and fluffy. Add the egg and cream cheese and mix again to combine. Sift in the flours (add any bran left in the sieve from the brown flour, if using), the cinnamon and salt and mix again. Fold in the toasted walnuts and the prunes with a large metal spoon.

Drop craggy mounds of the mixture onto the prepared baking trays – about 1 heaped dessertspoonful each. Leave room between them to allow the cookies to spread as they bake; 6 or 7 per baking tray is about right, so you will need to cook them in batches. Bake the cookies in the preheated oven for 10–12 minutes, or until golden. Leave to cool for a few minutes, then transfer to a wire rack to cool completely.

To make the cinnamon icing, sift the icing sugar and cinnamon into a small bowl. Add 2 teaspoons cold water and mix – you want a drizzling consistency, so add a few more drops of water if needed. Drizzle a little icing over each cookie and leave to set.

apricot, cherry and pine nut oat cookies

These are speedy and ideal to make with children, as the mixture won't come to any harm if it is rolled and prodded by little fingers. For a more grown-up variation, omit the cherries and add a level teaspoon of chopped fennel seeds with the oats.

50 g ready-to-eat dried apricots

50 g undyed glacé cherries

25 g pine nuts

100 g butter, softened

50 g light muscovado or light brown soft sugar

50 g plain flour

100 g porridge oats

2 baking trays, oiled

Makes about 18

Preheat the oven to 190°C (375°F) Gas 5.

Chop the apricots and cherries into small pieces and roughly chop the pine nuts.

Put the butter, sugar, flour and oats in an electric mixer (or use a large mixing bowl and an electric whisk) and beat until combined. Stir in the chopped apricots, cherries and pine nuts.

Bring the cookie dough together with your hands. Break off walnut-sized pieces and roll them into balls.

Arrange the balls of dough on the prepared baking trays and press each one to flatten it slightly. Bake the cookies in the preheated oven for 15–18 minutes, or until lightly golden. Transfer the cookies to a wire rack to cool.

mini peanut butter and maple refrigerator cookies

These small, chunky cookies are very simple to make. Once made and chilled, the dough will keep for a couple of weeks in the fridge, so you can bake the cookies as and when you need them. The dough also freezes well – defrost, then slice and bake.

175 g butter, softened and cubed

150 g crunchy peanut butter

2 tablespoons maple syrup

175 g light muscovado or light brown soft sugar

300 g plain flour, sifted

1 teaspoon baking powder

a pinch of salt

1 large egg, lightly beaten

Demerara sugar, for sprinkling

2–3 baking trays, oiled

Makes about 48

Put the butter, peanut butter, maple syrup and muscovado sugar in an electric mixer (or use a large mixing bowl and an electric whisk) and beat until combined. Tip in the flour, baking powder and salt and add the beaten egg. Beat to combine, then bring the dough together with your hands.

Tip the dough out onto a lightly floured surface and divide it into 4. Roll each quarter into a sausage shape about 16 cm in length and 3 cm in diameter. Wrap each one in clingfilm and refrigerate for 30 minutes. After that, when the cookie dough is firm, you can cut slices from it to bake as you wish.

To bake the cookies, preheat the oven to 200°C (400°F) Gas 6.

Slice 1½-cm thick circles of dough from the rolls; you should get about 12 cookies from each one.

Arrange the cookies on the prepared baking trays. Lightly press the back of a fork into the top of each cookie to make an indentation and sprinkle with Demerara sugar. Bake in the preheated oven for 10–12 minutes, or until golden. Leave to cool on wire racks.

salted caramel malt biscuits

If you don't have a cutter the right size to make these, cut around a glass, the lid of a small pot or similar. They are also cute made as mini-biscuits using a 3-cm cutter. The sea salt adds a special something to the caramel, making the biscuits dangerously moreish.

200 g self-raising flour

75 g malt powder, e.g. Horlicks

a tiny pinch of salt

150 g butter, softened and cubed

50 g caster sugar

1 medium egg, lightly beaten

Salted caramel

75 g dark muscovado or dark brown soft sugar

50 g butter

¼ teaspoon crushed sea salt, e.g. fleur de sel or Maldon

½ x 397-g tin condensed milk

a plain 5-cm cookie cutter

2 baking trays, oiled

Makes about 24

Sift the flour into the bowl of an electric mixer. Add the malt powder, salt and butter. Mix together until the mixture resembles breadcrumbs.

Tip in the sugar and the beaten egg. Mix until combined, then bring the dough together with your hands. Wrap in clingfilm and refrigerate for 30 minutes.

Preheat the oven to 190°C (375°F) Gas 5.

Tip half the dough out onto a lightly floured work surface and roll out until it is 8–9 mm thick. Using the cutter, stamp out rounds, then gently re-form the dough and continue until you have used it all.

Arrange the biscuits on the prepared baking trays. Bake in the preheated oven for 10 minutes, or until golden. Leave to cool on wire racks.

Repeat with the other half of the dough.

To make the salted caramel, gently heat the sugar, butter and sea salt in a pan until the sugar has dissolved, stirring now and then. Tip in the condensed milk and heat over low heat for 5–6 minutes, stirring all the time, until the mixture is amalgamated. Increase the heat, and as soon as the caramel starts to bubble, take the pan off the heat. Leave to cool until barely warm.

Top each biscuit with a swirl of the caramel, then leave to cool completely and set.

giant double chocolate chip cookies

Chewy and soft, these are a favourite to eat while still warm. I like chopping my own chocolate rather than using chocolate chips and often add a handful of roughly chopped unsalted shelled peanuts or hazelnuts too. If you want to make regular-sized cookies, just halve the size of the balls of dough that you bake.

225 g butter, softened

100 g light muscovado or light brown soft sugar

150 g Demerara sugar

2 large eggs, lightly beaten

300 g self-raising flour, sifted

½ teaspoon baking powder

a pinch of salt

125 g dark chocolate (about 50% cocoa solids)

125 g milk chocolate

2 baking trays, lined with baking parchment

Makes about 16

Preheat the oven to 180°C (350°F) Gas 4.

Put the butter and sugars in an electric mixer (or use a large mixing bowl and an electric whisk) and beat for 3–4 minutes, or until creamy and fluffy. Add the beaten eggs and mix again.

Tip in the flour, baking powder and salt and mix. Chop both types of chocolate into small chunks, then, using a large metal spoon, stir the chunks into the mixture. Break off golf ball-sized pieces and roll them into balls.

Arrange the balls of dough on the prepared baking trays. Leave room between them to allow the cookies to spread as they bake – they will end up being about 11–12 cm in diameter once cooked. You will need to cook them in batches. Bake in the preheated oven for 10–12 minutes, or until golden at the edges. Leave to cool for a couple of minutes, then transfer to a wire rack.

st. clement's macarons

Macarons have made a comeback in recent years and are now sold in all sorts of pretty colours. This is a simple way of making them and you can buy very good, luxury lemon or orange curd, which is ideal for filling them.

100 g ground almonds

150 g caster sugar

2 teaspoons plain flour

2 large egg whites

grated zest of 1 unwaxed lemon

grated zest of ½ orange

Filling

3 tablespoons cream cheese

3 tablespoons thick lemon or orange curd

grated zest of ½ orange

2 baking trays, lined with baking parchment

Makes 12

Preheat the oven to 180°C (350°F) Gas 4.

Tip all the ingredients (other than those for the filling) into an electric mixer. Alternatively, put them in a large mixing bowl and use an electric whisk. Beat together until well combined.

Put 24 teaspoonfuls of the mixture onto the prepared baking trays, leaving room for them to spread slightly. Bake in the preheated oven for 15–17 minutes, or until set and tinged with gold at the edges. Leave to cool for a few minutes, then transfer to wire racks.

To make the filling, whisk the cream cheese and curd together until smooth. Stir in the orange zest and refrigerate until needed. Sandwich the macarons together with the filling.

dark chocolate thins with white chocolate filling

These delicate but very chocolatey biscuits have a thin layer of sweet filling. If you want to cheat, fill them with hazelnut chocolate spread instead.

125 g butter, softened

50 g caster sugar

150 g plain flour, sifted

25 g cocoa powder, plus extra for dusting

75 g dark chocolate (about 50% cocoa solids), broken into pieces

1 tablespoon vegetable oil

White chocolate filling

75 g white chocolate, broken into pieces

2 teaspoons runny honey

2 tablespoons crème fraîche

2 baking trays, lined with baking parchment

Makes 10

Put the butter and sugar in an electric mixer (or use a large mixing bowl and an electric whisk) and beat until light and fluffy. Tip in the flour and cocoa and mix to combine. If the mixture doesn't come together straightaway, work it briefly with a spatula, then mix again until it comes together in a ball. Wrap in clingfilm and refrigerate for 30 minutes.

To make the white chocolate filling, put the chocolate pieces, honey and crème fraîche in a small heatproof bowl set over a pan of barely simmering water. Stir until the chocolate has melted and the mixture is smooth. Take the bowl off the heat, leave to cool, then refrigerate.

Preheat the oven to 160°C (325°F) Gas 3.

Lightly dust a work surface with cocoa. Halve the chilled dough and roll one half out on the work surface until it is about 5 mm thick. Cut out 10 rectangles, 7 x 4 cm, re-rolling the dough as necessary. Arrange the biscuits on one baking tray. Repeat with the other half of the dough.

Bake in the preheated oven for 10 minutes. Leave to cool for a few minutes, then transfer to wire racks.

Melt the dark chocolate with the oil in the same way you melted the white chocolate above. Take the bowl off the heat and dip the opposite corners of half the biscuits into it. Leave to set.

Bring the filling back to room temperature and give it a stir. Spread a layer of filling on the underside of each of the plain biscuits and place a chocolate-dipped biscuit on top.

passion-fruit biscuit sandwiches

These are dainty, melt-in-the-mouth biscuits sandwiched together with a passion-fruit cream. Choose passion fruit that have wrinkled skins, as they will be the most fragrant and juicy.

500 g butter, softened

100 g icing sugar, sifted, plus extra for dusting

400 g plain flour, sifted

100 g cornflour, sifted

Passion-fruit cream

100 g mascarpone

75 g icing sugar, sifted

pulp of 2 passion fruit

a piping bag, fitted with a wide plain or star nozzle

3 baking trays, lined with baking parchment

Makes 14

Preheat the oven to 180°C (350°F) Gas 4.

Put the butter and sugar in an electric mixer (or use a large mixing bowl and an electric whisk) and beat together until pale and creamy. Tip in the flour and cornflour and whisk again to combine.

Fill the piping bag with the mixture and use to pipe 9-cm lengths onto the prepared baking trays. Leave room between them to allow the biscuits to spread as they bake. Bake in the preheated oven for 15–18 minutes, or until lightly golden at the edges. Leave to cool on the baking trays.

To make the passion-fruit cream, mix all the ingredients together and refrigerate until needed.

Sandwich the biscuits together with the passion-fruit cream. Lightly dust the top of each one with icing sugar.

bright-as-a-button biscuits

These are fun to make and children will enjoy the brightly coloured icings. Experiment with different food colours or you can, of course, ice them all one colour. Alternatively, leave them plain, if you prefer.

Put the butter and sugar in an electric mixer (or use a large mixing bowl and an electric whisk) and beat together until pale and fluffy. Add the beaten egg, flour, ground almonds, baking powder and lemon juice and mix to combine.

Tip the dough onto a lightly floured work surface and bring it together in a ball. Press the ball into a disc, wrap in clingfilm and refrigerate for at least 30 minutes.

Preheat the oven to 200°C (400°F) Gas 6.

Halve the chilled dough and roll one half out on the lightly floured work surface until it is about 5 mm thick. Cut out 5 x 10-cm circles, using an upturned tea cup or similar to cut around. Arrange the biscuits on one of the prepared baking trays. Using the

1½-cm cookie cutter (or the tip of a small sharp knife), stamp out 2 rounds from the middle of each biscuit to make buttonholes.

Repeat with the other half of the dough. Bake in the preheated oven for 10 minutes. Transfer to wire racks to cool.

To decorate, sift the icing sugar into a bowl and stir in 3–4 tablespoons cold water – add it little by little until you have a thick icing consistency; you may not need it all. Divide the icing between 3 bowls and add a touch of food colouring to each. Add it with the very tip of a small knife – you really don't need much. Mix thoroughly.

Spread icing on each of the buttons. Leave to set for about 30 minutes before threading ribbon through the buttonholes.

100 g butter, softened and cubed

100 g caster sugar

1 large egg, lightly beaten

175 g plain flour

100 g ground almonds

1 teaspoon baking powder

4 teaspoons freshly squeezed lemon juice

To decorate

400 g icing sugar

food colouring pastes or liquid colours – hot pink, orange, yellow and green work well together

2 large baking trays, lined with baking parchment

a 1½-cm plain cookie cutter (optional)

3 m thin–medium ribbon

Makes 10

spiced brown sugar and clementine stars

These crisp, spiced biscuits are pretty baked as stars but you can experiment with other shapes – hearts are cute too. If you are making them to hang on a Christmas tree, as soon as they come out of the oven make holes at one end of each biscuit using a skewer, to thread ribbon through later.

100 g butter, softened and cubed

75 g dark muscovado or dark brown soft sugar

1 teaspoon golden syrup

1 medium egg, lightly beaten

200 g plain flour, sifted

1 teaspoon baking powder

grated zest of 1 clementine

2 teaspoons ground cinnamon

a generous pinch each of ground nutmeg, allspice and cloves

To decorate

100 g icing sugar

6–7 teaspoons freshly squeezed lemon juice

edible silver balls

edible white glitter

star cookie cutters in various sizes

2 large baking trays, lined with baking parchment

Makes about 30

Put the butter, sugar and golden syrup in an electric mixer (or use a large mixing bowl and an electric whisk) and mix until combined. Add the beaten egg little by little, alternating with a spoonful of flour, and still mixing. Add the rest of the flour, the baking powder, clementine zest and spices. Mix to combine.

Tip the dough onto a lightly floured work surface and bring it together in a ball. Press the ball into a disc, wrap in clingfilm and refrigerate for at least 30 minutes.

Preheat the oven to 200°C (400°F) Gas 6.

Halve the chilled dough and roll one half out on the lightly floured work surface until it is about 5 mm thick. Cut out stars with the cookie cutters and arrange the biscuits on one of the prepared baking trays. Gently re-form and re-roll the dough, then keep stamping out stars.

Repeat with the other half of the dough. Bake in the preheated oven for 8–10 minutes for smaller stars (about 6 cm) and 12–14 minutes for larger stars (about 8.5 cm). When they are ready, the dough will have risen slightly and the edges will be tinged with brown. Transfer to wire racks to cool.

To decorate, sift the icing sugar into a bowl and stir in the lemon juice – add it little by little until you have a drizzling consistency. Decorate each star with a little icing (you can pipe it if you are feeling fancy). Finish with edible silver balls and glitter.

gingerbread men

The gingerbread men are crisp when baked, so are pretty resilient for children to ice them with tubes of ready-made icing, if that should appeal.

100 g butter

50 g dark muscovado or dark brown soft sugar

225 g plain flour

¾ teaspoon bicarbonate of soda

2 teaspoons ground ginger

1 teaspoon ground cinnamon

4 tablespoons golden syrup

1 tablespoon black treacle

small coloured sugar-coated chocolate drops or halved currants, for decoration

a 7–8-cm (top to bottom) gingerbread man cutter

2 baking trays, lightly buttered

Makes about 18

Heat the butter and sugar together in a small pan until melted, stirring every now and then. Remove the pan from the heat and leave to cool slightly.

Sift the flour, bicarbonate of soda, and ground ginger and cinnamon into the bowl of an electric mixer (or use a large mixing bowl and an electric whisk) and pour the melted butter mixture into it. Add the golden syrup and treacle and mix to combine. Bring together into a ball, wrap in clingfilm and refrigerate for 30 minutes.

Preheat the oven to 190°C (375°F) Gas 5.

Halve the chilled dough and roll one half out on the lightly floured work surface until it is about 5–6 mm thick. Cut out men with the cutter and arrange the biscuits on one of the prepared baking trays. Gently re-form and re-roll the dough, then keep stamping out gingerbread men. Make indentations for eyes and mouths and add sugar-coated chocolate drops or currants for buttons.

Repeat with the other half of the dough.

Bake the gingerbread men in the preheated oven for 8 minutes, or until they are set and slightly firmer to the touch. Transfer to wire racks to cool.

tray
bakes
& bars

hazelnut cheesecake bars

These bars will keep in the fridge for a day or so. They are ideal for coffee time or they also double up well as a simple pudding with poached fruit alongside.

200 g shelled, blanched whole hazelnuts

75 g butter

200 g ginger nut biscuits, broken into pieces

icing sugar, for dusting

Cheesecake topping

400 g cream cheese

175 g caster sugar

3 large eggs

300 ml soured cream

a 20 x 33 x 3–4-cm baking tin, oiled

Makes 14

Preheat the oven to 180°C (350°F) Gas 4.

Spread the hazelnuts on a baking tray and toast in the preheated oven for 10–12 minutes, then leave to cool. Reduce the oven temperature to 160°C (325°F) Gas 3.

Melt the butter in a small pan and leave to cool slightly.

Tip the biscuits into a food processor. Add half the cooled hazelnuts and whiz together until you have fine crumbs. Add the melted butter and briefly whiz again. Tip the mixture into the prepared baking tin and press down firmly with the back of a spoon to make an even layer. Put the tin on a baking tray.

To make the cheesecake topping, put all the ingredients in an electric mixer (or use a large mixing bowl and an electric whisk) and whisk to combine. Carefully pour the mixture on top of the biscuit base in the tin – the mixture will come pretty near the top. Roughly chop the remaining hazelnuts and scatter over the cheesecake. Bake in the preheated oven for 45 minutes. Leave to cool completely.

Refrigerate for 30 minutes before cutting into 14 bars with a sharp knife. The cheesecake will be soft-set. Lightly dust with icing sugar.

chocolate fudge raspberry shortbread bars

This is a sophisticated, bite-sized number; the tart fruitiness of the raspberries complements the dark chocolate.

125 g butter, softened

50 g granulated sugar

150 g plain flour

Chocolate topping

400 ml double cream

2 tablespoons icing sugar

400 g dark chocolate (70% cocoa solids), broken into small pieces

200 g raspberries

a 20-cm square tin, ideally loose-based, oiled

Makes 21

Preheat the oven to 190°C (375°F) Gas 5.

Put the butter and sugar in an electric mixer and beat for 3–4 minutes, or until pale and creamy. Tip in the flour and mix again for a few minutes to combine – the dough probably won't come together in a ball, but if you work it briefly with a wooden spoon and then your hands, it will come together. Tip into the prepared tin and press down firmly with the back of a spoon to make an even layer. Prick the base a few times with a fork. Bake in the preheated oven for 20 minutes, or until lightly golden. Leave to cool.

To make the chocolate topping, bring the cream and icing sugar slowly to the boil in a pan. Put the chocolate pieces in a heatproof bowl. As soon as the cream begins to bubble, remove from the heat and pour into the bowl with the chocolate. Gently whisk together until the chocolate has melted and the mixture is smooth.

Stir the raspberries into the chocolate mixture, then pour it over the cooled biscuit base. Leave to cool completely, then refrigerate for 3 hours, or until set. Cut into 21 bars with a sharp knife.

pecan cheesecake swirl brownies

These brownies are gorgeous to look at and won't disappoint any brownie lover. Don't overcook them, as you want them to have slightly squidgy centres.

100 g pecan halves

100 g dark chocolate
(70% cocoa solids),
broken into pieces

100 g butter, softened

200 g light muscovado or
light brown soft sugar

2 large eggs, lightly beaten

100 g plain flour, sifted

Cheesecake swirl

1 large egg

150 g cream cheese

40 g granulated sugar

1 tablespoon plain flour

an 18-cm square tin,
oiled and base-lined with
baking parchment

Makes 16

Preheat the oven to 180°C (350°F) Gas 4.

Spread the pecans on a baking tray and toast in the preheated oven for 10 minutes, then leave to cool.

Melt the chocolate pieces in a small heatproof bowl set over a pan of barely simmering water. Remove the bowl from the heat and leave to cool a little.

Roughly chop the toasted pecans.

Put the butter and sugar in an electric mixer (or use a large mixing bowl and an electric whisk) and beat until combined. Gradually add the beaten eggs, still mixing. Tip in the flour and add the slightly cooled melted chocolate. Mix again until combined. Using a large metal spoon, fold in the chopped pecans.

To make the cheesecake swirl, whisk all the ingredients together in a bowl until combined.

Tip the chocolate mixture into the prepared tin and spread it evenly with a spatula. Drop blobs of the cheesecake mixture on top and, using a skewer or the end of a teaspoon, briefly swirl the cheesecake mixture into the top of the chocolate layer.

Bake the brownies in the preheated oven for 25 minutes. Leave to cool completely before cutting into 16 squares.

spiced date, apple and treacle oat slices

My mother used to make these for me when I was revising for school exams, so we called them exam slices. I still love them.

250 g stoned, soft dates, chopped

2 tart dessert apples, cored, peeled and chopped

finely grated zest of 1 orange

freshly squeezed juice of 2 oranges

1 teaspoon freshly squeezed lemon juice

1 teaspoon mixed spice

Treacle oat layer

100 g porridge oats

100 g caster sugar

100 g self-raising flour

50 g butter, softened and cubed

50 g golden syrup

1 large egg yolk

an 18-cm square tin, ideally loose-based, oiled

Makes 10

Tip the chopped dates, apples, orange zest and juice, lemon juice and mixed spice into a medium pan. Mix and heat over medium heat. Once everything has come to simmering point, reduce the heat to low and gently cook the fruit for 8–10 minutes, covered, until the apple has softened. Leave to cool.

Preheat the oven to 180°C (350°F) Gas 4.

To make the treacle oat layer, put all the ingredients in an electric mixer (or use a large mixing bowl and an electric whisk) and beat to combine. Tip half this mixture into the base of the prepared tin and press down firmly with the back of a spoon to make an even layer.

Spoon the cooled date and apple mixture on top of the treacle oat base and top with the remaining treacle oat layer, pressing it down again to make an even layer. Bake in the preheated oven for 30 minutes. Leave to cool completely before cutting into 10 bars.

coconut, apricot and lime slices

These are a modern version of the coconut slice. The traditional version has raspberry jam beneath the coconut topping, but I think these are all the better for their juicy apricot layer.

125 g butter, softened

50 g Demerara sugar

150 g plain flour

450 g ready-to-eat dried apricots, finely chopped

grated zest and freshly squeezed juice of 3 limes

Coconut topping

2 large eggs

1 x 160-ml tin coconut cream

50 g caster sugar

125 g desiccated coconut

a 20 x 33-cm baking tin, 3–4 cm deep, oiled

Makes 14

Preheat the oven to 180°C (350°F) Gas 4.

Put the butter and sugar in an electric mixer and beat for 3–4 minutes, or until pale and creamy. Tip in the flour and mix again for a few minutes to combine.

Tip the mixture into the prepared tin and press down firmly with the back of a spoon to make an even layer. Prick the base a few times with a fork. Bake in the preheated oven for 15–20 minutes, or until lightly golden. Leave the oven on.

Meanwhile, put the apricots and lime zest and juice in a medium pan with 4 tablespoons cold water and bring to simmering point. Gently cook, covered, for 8–10 minutes, or until soft and mushy. Add another tablespoon of water if the mixture seems too dry as it simmers. Leave the apricots to cool slightly, then transfer to a food processor and whiz to a thick purée.

To make the coconut topping, lightly beat the eggs in the electric mixer, then add the coconut cream, sugar and desiccated coconut and mix to combine.

Spread the apricot purée on top of the baked base and top with the coconut mixture, spreading it evenly. Bake for 40–45 minutes, or until golden. Leave to cool completely before cutting into 14 slices.

cherry marzipan streusel squares

These are also a favourite when made with raspberry or plum jam.

100 g plain flour

50 g butter, chilled
and diced

1 tablespoon icing sugar

5 tablespoons morello
cherry jam

Streusel topping

75 g plain flour

75 g granulated sugar

25 g butter, softened
and cubed

50 g marzipan, diced

50 g undyed glacé cherries,
chopped

50 g flaked almonds

Almond layer

100 g butter, softened
and cubed

75 g caster sugar

2 large eggs, lightly beaten

100 g ground almonds

25 g plain flour

*an 18-cm square tin, ideally
loose-based, oiled*

Makes 12

For the pastry, put the flour, butter and sugar in an electric mixer and whiz until the mixture resembles breadcrumbs. Add 2 tablespoons cold water and whiz again. Add a few more drops of water, if needed, to bring together into a dough.

Tip the pastry out on a lightly floured work surface and roll out until it is about 3–4 mm thick. Trim the edges with a sharp knife to make a 19-cm square. Line the base of the tin with the pastry – it will come slightly up the inside of the tin all the way round. Refrigerate for 30 minutes.

Preheat the oven to 200°C (400°F) Gas 6.

To make the streusel topping, tip the flour and sugar into the electric mixer (or use a mixing bowl and an electric whisk) and whiz together. Add the butter and whiz until the mixture is crumbly. Tip into a bowl, if necessary, and stir in the marzipan, glacé cherries and flaked almonds.

To make the almond layer, mix all the ingredients together in the electric mixer until amalgamated.

Spread the cherry jam on top of the chilled pastry base. Spoon blobs of the almond mixture on top of the jam and spread them out with a spatula. Scatter the streusel topping over the top. Put the tin on a baking tray and bake in the preheated oven for 40 minutes, or until lightly golden. Cover with foil towards the end of cooking to prevent over-browning. Leave to cool in the tin before cutting into 12 squares.

throw-together muesli bars

These are a really quick assembly job and will keep in an airtight container for several days, and they freeze well too. Perfect for picnics, long walks and lunchboxes.

100 g butter

4 tablespoons golden syrup

75 g caster sugar

225 g jumbo rolled oats

125 g ready-to-eat dried apricots, chopped

100 g stoned, soft dates, chopped

4 tablespoons sultanas

4 tablespoons chopped pistachios

3 tablespoons chopped brazil nuts

3 tablespoons sesame seeds

1 tablespoon freshly squeezed lemon juice

a 20-cm square tin, ideally loose-based, well oiled

Makes 8

Preheat the oven to 190°C (375°F) Gas 5.

Heat the butter and golden syrup together in a small pan until melted.

Meanwhile, combine all the other ingredients in a large mixing bowl. Add the warm butter mixture and stir thoroughly to combine.

Tip the mixture into the prepared tin and press down firmly with the back of a spoon to make an even layer. Bake in the preheated oven for 25 minutes, or until golden. Leave to cool for 15 minutes or so, then, using a sharp knife, carefully cut into 8 bars. Leave to cool completely before lifting the bars out of the tin.

nectarine and blueberry tray bake with lavender sugar

This tray bake is packed full of juicy fruit. You can leave out the lavender if it isn't your thing and the nectarines can be swapped for peaches, a similar quantity of plums or apricots, or 250 g mixed berries. In any case, the tray bake is best made and eaten on the same day.

3 large eggs

200 g caster sugar

175 g self-raising flour, sifted

1 teaspoon baking powder

½ teaspoon vanilla extract

175 g butter, softened and cubed

½ tablespoon dried lavender buds

3 ripe but firm nectarines

200 g blueberries

1 tablespoon polenta (cornmeal)

Lavender sugar

½ tablespoon dried lavender buds

2 tablespoons caster sugar

grated zest of 1 unwaxed lemon

a 20 x 33-cm baking tin, 3–4 cm deep, lined with baking parchment and lightly buttered

Serves 14

Preheat the oven to 180°C (350°F) Gas 4.

Put the eggs, sugar, flour, baking powder, vanilla extract, butter and lavender in an electric mixer (or use a large mixing bowl and an electric whisk) and whisk together. Stone the nectarines, chop them into bite-sized pieces and stir into the mixture along with the blueberries.

Dust the bottom of the prepared tin with the polenta and a very small amount of flour. Spoon the mixture into the tin and spread it evenly with a spatula.

To make the lavender sugar, mix the ingredients together in a bowl, then scatter evenly over the tray bake.

Bake in the preheated oven for 35 minutes, or until risen and golden. Leave to cool in the tin before cutting into 14 rectangles.

sticky toffee tray bake with toffee fudge drizzle

Another day, try replacing the ginger with 50 g sultanas in the mix and use golden syrup in the icing instead of the ginger syrup. Both versions always seem to vanish very quickly.

175 g butter, softened

125 g dark muscovado or dark brown soft sugar

150 g golden syrup

75 g black treacle

200 g self-raising flour

1 teaspoon vanilla extract

3 large eggs

2 tablespoons double cream

2 balls stem ginger in syrup, drained and finely chopped

Toffee fudge icing

50 g butter

1 tablespoon of the syrup from the jar of stem ginger

2 tablespoons double cream

75 g dark muscovado or dark brown soft sugar

40 g icing sugar

a 20 x 33-cm baking tin, 3–4 cm deep, lined with baking parchment and lightly buttered

Serves 14

Preheat the oven to 180°C (350°F) Gas 4.

Put the butter, sugar, golden syrup, treacle, flour, vanilla extract, eggs and cream in an electric mixer (or use a large mixing bowl and an electric whisk) and beat until combined. Stir in the stem ginger.

Tip the mixture into the prepared tin and spread it evenly with a spatula. Bake in the preheated oven for 25–30 minutes, or until risen and just set in the middle. Leave to cool completely in the tin.

To make the toffee fudge icing, put the butter, ginger syrup, cream and muscovado sugar in a medium pan over low heat and leave until the butter has melted and the sugar dissolved. Remove the pan from the heat, sift in the icing sugar, then whisk it in.

Remove the cake from the tin and drizzle the icing over it. Leave to set before cutting the tray bake into 14 slices.

lemon squares

These look pretty as they are, lightly dusted with icing sugar, but I sometimes top each square with a slice of fig or strawberry too.

100 g plain flour

35 g icing sugar, plus extra for dusting

75 g unsalted butter, chilled and cubed

1–2 figs, very thinly sliced, to decorate (optional)

Lemon layer

3 large eggs

275 g caster sugar

finely grated zest of 1 unwaxed lemon

150 ml freshly squeezed lemon juice (from 3–4 lemons)

50 g plain flour, sifted

an 18-cm square tin, oiled

Makes 16

Preheat the oven to 180°C (350°F) Gas 4.

First prepare the tin. Place 2 wide strips of baking parchment from one side to the other of the tin so that they form a cross on the base – this will help you to lift the cake out of the tin when it is cooked. Place a square of baking parchment on top of the strips, as you would usually do to line the base of a tin.

Put the flour, icing sugar and butter in an electric mixer (or use a large mixing bowl and an electric whisk) and whiz until the mixture resembles breadcrumbs. Tip the mixture into the prepared tin and press down firmly with the back of a spoon to make an even layer. Prick the base a few times with a fork. Bake in the preheated oven for 12–15 minutes, or until lightly golden. Reduce the oven temperature to 150°C (300°F) Gas 3.

To make the lemon layer, put the eggs, sugar and lemon zest in the electric mixer and beat for a minute or so. With the beaters still going, gradually pour in the lemon juice, then tip in the flour and mix to combine.

Tip the mixture on top of the baked base. Bake for 45 minutes, by which time the lemon layer will be set and the top slightly crusty. Leave to cool completely.

Run a sharp knife around the edges, then lift out of the tin. Lightly dust with icing sugar and cut into 16 squares. Decorate with the thin slices of fig, if using.

in a flash

lime drizzle cake with coconut frosting

If you want to make this look extra special, add a few shavings of toasted fresh coconut to the top.

175 g butter, softened

175 g caster sugar

175 g self-raising flour, sifted

3 eggs

finely grated zest of 2 limes

Lime drizzle

75 g icing sugar

freshly squeezed juice of 2 limes

Coconut frosting

175 g cream cheese

5 tablespoons coconut cream

2 tablespoons icing sugar

grated zest of 1 lime (use a zester, if you have one, rather than a fine grater)

an 18-cm round tin, 7 cm deep, lightly buttered and base-lined with baking parchment

Serves 8

Preheat the oven to 180°C (350°F) Gas 4.

Put the butter, sugar, flour, eggs and lime zest in an electric mixer (or use a large mixing bowl and an electric whisk) and beat until combined.

Spoon the mixture into the prepared tin and spread it evenly with a spatula. Bake in the preheated oven for 50–55 minutes, or until a skewer comes out clean when inserted into the centre of the cake.

Meanwhile, to make the lime drizzle, sift the icing sugar into a bowl and stir in the lime juice, then set aside.

To make the coconut frosting, whisk the cream cheese, coconut cream and icing sugar together in a bowl, then refrigerate until needed.

When the cake is ready, remove it from the oven and, using a small, fine skewer, make a few holes over the surface of the cake. Spoon over the lime drizzle (put the tin on a plate first if it is loose-based). Leave the cake to cool completely in its tin.

Once cold, pop the cake out of the tin, remove the base paper and spread the frosting over the top. Sprinkle with the lime zest.

simple fruit cake

This energy-giving cut-and-come-again cake is full of fruit and nuts and uses agave nectar – a low-GI, natural fructose sweetener – so a slice will keep hunger at bay. Agave nectar is now available in many supermarkets. If you want to make this cake more celebratory, brush warm, smooth apricot jam over it and decorate with small dried apricots and pecan halves.

100 g ready-to-eat dried apricots or figs

125 g stoned, soft Agen prunes

125 g shelled pecan nuts, almonds, hazelnuts or walnuts, or a mixture

150 g butter, softened

125 g light brown soft sugar

175 g self-raising flour

1 teaspoon ground cinnamon

3 large eggs, lightly beaten

150 g sultanas

juice and zest of 1 orange

juice and zest of 1 unwaxed lemon

2 tablespoons agave nectar (or runny honey)

2 pure cane rough-cut sugar cubes, roughly crushed

an 18-cm square tin, 7 cm deep, lined with baking parchment and buttered

Serves 12

Preheat the oven to 150°C (300°F) Gas 2.

Using scissors, snip the dried apricots and the prunes into small pieces. Roughly chop the nuts.

Put the butter and sugar in an electric mixer (or use a large mixing bowl and an electric whisk) and beat until combined and fluffy.

Sift the flour and cinnamon into another bowl.

Add the flour mixture and beaten eggs alternately to the butter and sugar, whisking on a low setting all the time.

Using a large metal or wooden spoon, stir in the chopped fruit and nuts, the sultanas, orange and lemon juices and zests and the agave nectar. Mix well.

Tip the mixture into the prepared tin and spread it evenly with a spatula. Sprinkle the crushed sugar over the cake, then bake in the preheated oven for 1¼ hours. Leave to cool in the tin.

blackcurrant, berry and hazelnut crumble cake

This recipe also works well using damson jam. Either way, treat yourself to some chilled Greek yoghurt on the side.

150 g butter, softened

175 g caster sugar

2 large eggs

125 g self-raising flour

50 g polenta (cornmeal)

1 teaspoon baking powder

finely grated zest of
1 small unwaxed lemon

50 g authentic Greek yoghurt

175 g blackcurrant jam

175 g raspberries

Crumble topping

100 g shelled, blanched
whole hazelnuts

75 g Demerara sugar

75 g butter, chilled and
cubed

100 g self-raising flour

*a 23-cm springform tin, 6 cm
deep, lightly buttered and
base-lined with baking
parchment*

Serves 12

Preheat the oven to 180°C (350°F) Gas 4.

To make the crumble topping, chop the nuts by hand or pulse them in a food processor – you want them to be roughly chopped. Mix the sugar, butter and flour in an electric mixer until combined, then add 2 dessertspoons cold water and briefly whiz again until the mixture resembles breadcrumbs. Mix in the nuts. Alternatively, you can rub the butter into the flour by hand in a mixing bowl, then stir in the sugar, water and nuts. Set aside.

Put the butter, sugar, eggs, flour, polenta, baking powder, lemon zest and Greek yoghurt in an electric mixer and mix until combined.

Spoon the mixture into the prepared tin and spread it evenly. Tip the jam into a bowl and mix it with a spoon to loosen it, then put spoonfuls over the top of the cake mixture. Using the tip of a round-bladed knife, gently spread the jam by lightly swirling it into the top of the cake mixture. Sprinkle a third of the crumble mixture on top, scatter the raspberries over this, then finish with the remaining crumble topping.

Put the tin on a baking tray and bake in the preheated oven for 1 hour 5 minutes–1 hour 10 minutes, until just set in the middle. Leave to cool in the tin before releasing it, removing the base paper and transferring to a plate or board to slice.

mocha swirl loaf with espresso icing

The fromage frais in this loaf keeps the fat content down and the polenta gives it a lovely crunchy crust.

1 slightly rounded tablespoon espresso instant coffee powder

1 tablespoon boiling water

200 g fromage frais

75 g polenta (cornmeal)

125 g butter, softened

225 g caster sugar

3 large eggs

200 g self-raising flour

½ teaspoon bicarbonate of soda

1 teaspoon vanilla extract

2 teaspoons cocoa powder

Espresso icing

100 g icing sugar

1 slightly rounded teaspoon espresso instant coffee powder

a 19 x 9-cm loaf tin, 7 cm deep, lightly buttered and base-lined with baking parchment

Serves 8-10

Preheat the oven to 180°C (350°F) Gas 4.

Put the espresso powder and boiling water in a cup and stir to dissolve, then leave to cool.

Next, take a scant tablespoon from the fromage frais and set it aside for the icing. Put the remaining fromage frais with the polenta, butter, sugar, eggs, flour and bicarbonate of soda in an electric mixer (or use a large mixing bowl and an electric whisk) and beat until combined. Transfer half the mixture to another bowl. Stir the vanilla extract into the first bowl. Stir the dissolved coffee and the cocoa into the second bowl.

Spoon the 2 mixtures into the prepared loaf tin in 3 layers, alternating spoonfuls of each mixture in each layer to resemble a chequerboard. Finally, using a skewer, gently swirl the layers together a few times until you have a definite swirl pattern on top of the loaf.

Bake in the preheated oven for 55 minutes, or until risen and the loaf is a lovely golden colour on top. Leave to cool in the tin.

To make the espresso icing, sift the icing sugar into a bowl and mix in the espresso powder along with the reserved tablespoon of fromage frais. Add enough cold water to make the icing a spreadable consistency – about 2 teaspoonfuls – but add it gradually, stirring, as you might not need it all.

Run a knife around the edges of the cold loaf in the tin to release it. Turn it out, remove the base paper and spread the icing on top of the loaf. Leave to set before slicing.

almond cake

This is delicious as is or eaten with baked rhubarb – cut rhubarb into chunks, sprinkle generously with sugar and bake at the same temperature as the cake for 15–20 minutes, or until just soft, then leave to cool. Buy ready-toasted flaked almonds to make this cake extra speedy to decorate.

225 g caster sugar

150 g butter, softened and cubed

4 large eggs

1 teaspoon almond extract

75 g self-raising flour

1 rounded teaspoon baking powder

125 g ground almonds

To finish

100 g icing sugar

freshly squeezed juice of 1 small lemon

2 tablespoons toasted flaked almonds

an 18-cm round, loose-based tin, 7 cm deep, lightly buttered and base-lined with baking parchment

Serves 8

Preheat the oven to 180°C (350°F) Gas 4.

Put all the ingredients for the cake in an electric mixer (or use a large mixing bowl and an electric whisk) and beat until combined.

Pour the mixture into the prepared tin and spread it evenly with a spatula. Put the tin on a baking tray and bake in the preheated oven for 40 minutes, or until golden and firm to the touch in the centre. Leave the cake to cool in the tin.

Tip the cold cake out of the tin and remove the baking parchment. Place on a wire rack over a board.

To finish, sift the icing sugar into a bowl and stir in the lemon juice, little by little. You probably won't need it all – you are aiming for a thick pouring icing. Spoon the icing over the cake, letting it drizzle down the side of the cake. Scatter the flaked almonds on the top.

crunchy prune and vanilla custard brioche cakes

These individual cakes have an indulgent fruity custard hiding under their crunchy topping. They are also good made with limoncello instead of the brandy, but leave out the alcohol altogether if you prefer. Use the thick custard you can buy in cartons from the supermarket, and if time is really short, use muffin cases instead of making your own liners. These are best eaten on the day they are made.

2 large eggs

2 tablespoons Armagnac or other brandy

4 tablespoons Demerara sugar

½ teaspoon vanilla extract

250 g thick ready-made custard

75 g butter

200 g brioche

100 g stoned, soft Agen prunes, snipped into small pieces

a 6-hole muffin tin, each hole well buttered and lined with a 17-cm square of baking parchment

Makes 6

Preheat the oven to 180°C (350°F) Gas 4.

In a large measuring jug and using a balloon whisk, whisk together the eggs, Armagnac, 1 tablespoon of the sugar, the vanilla extract and the custard.

Melt the butter in a small pan and pour into a large mixing bowl.

Cut the brioche into 1–1½-cm squares. Toss the squares in the melted butter with 2 tablespoons of the sugar, mixing well. Divide half the squares between the parchment-lined holes in the muffin tin, pressing them down firmly to make a base.

Divide the prune pieces between each muffin, then do the same with the custard mixture. Now add the rest of the brioche squares to the muffins, piling it up high. Scatter the remaining sugar over the top.

Bake in the preheated oven for 35 minutes, or until set and golden on top. Eat warm or cold.

no-bake chocolate, macadamia and fig slices

These are as simple as can be and delicious with an espresso on the side. If you want to make them less sophisticated, for children, you can replace the macadamia nuts with any other type of nut and the dried figs with raisins or dried apricots.

100 g unsalted butter

2 tablespoons runny honey

300 g dark chocolate (50–70% cocoa solids), broken into pieces

100 g milk chocolate, broken into pieces

100 g digestive or other sweetmeal biscuits

100 g shelled macadamia nuts

100 g ready-to-eat dried figs

cocoa powder, for dusting

an 18-cm square tin, ideally loose-based, oiled

Makes 16

Put the butter, honey and both types of chocolate in a medium pan and melt gently, stirring from time to time.

Meanwhile, roughly chop the biscuits, nuts and figs. Stir into the melted chocolate mixture.

Tip the mixture into the prepared tin. Leave to cool completely before refrigerating for 2–3 hours to set. Cut into 16 slices.

peach, vanilla and cherry shortcake

This is such a pretty option for a summer tea in the garden. Strawberries and raspberries also make a nice topping with a little shredded lemon verbena or, in the autumn, thin slices of baked quince, a handful of blackberries and a scattering of toasted nuts.

100 g plain flour

75 g butter, softened and cubed

40 g icing sugar, sifted

1 medium egg yolk

Topping

1 vanilla pod, split lengthways

125 ml double or whipping cream, chilled

2 tablespoons icing sugar, plus extra for dusting

2 ripe but firm peaches, stoned and sliced

100 g cherries, stoned and halved

a squeeze of lemon juice

2 tablespoons shredded basil leaves

a baking tray, lined with baking parchment

Serves 4

Put the flour, butter, sugar and egg yolk in a food processor and mix together. If the dough doesn't come together, tip it into a bowl and work it with a spatula. Alternatively, you can make it by hand to start with. Tip the dough onto a lightly floured work surface and bring it together in a ball. Press the ball into a disc, wrap in clingfilm and refrigerate for 15 minutes.

Preheat the oven to 190°C (375°F) Gas 5.

Tip the dough out onto the lightly floured surface and roll or pat it out until it is big enough to cut out a 15-cm round – I use a plate or upturned bowl to cut around.

Transfer the round to the prepared baking tray and bake in the preheated oven for 10–12 minutes, or until set and lightly golden at the edges. Leave to cool completely.

To make the topping, scrape the seeds out of the vanilla pod and into a bowl with the cream and half the icing sugar. Whip into soft peaks.

Toss the sliced peaches and halved cherries with the lemon juice, basil and the remaining icing sugar.

Dust the cold shortcake lightly with more icing sugar, then top with the cream mixture and scatter the fruit mixture over the top. Serve immediately.

chocolate snaps with ricotta, pistachios and candied fruit

These are easy but impressive and the flavours are similar to those of Sicilian *cannoli*. For a variation, try moulding some of the baked rounds into tubes – use rounded teaspoonfuls of the mixture and bake in the same way. If you leave the rounds on the tray to cool, as below, they are easy to remove and curl around the base of a wooden spoon or by hand. Bake just a few at a time and fill them with the same ricotta filling.

50 g butter

50 g Demerara sugar

50 g golden syrup

40 g plain flour

10 g cocoa powder, plus extra for dusting

a pinch of salt

Filling

250 g ricotta, chilled

1 tablespoon icing sugar

50 g shelled, unsalted pistachios, finely chopped

50 g dark chocolate (70% cocoa solids), finely chopped

25 g chopped mixed candied peel

1 teaspoon orange flower water

a large baking tray, lined with baking parchment

Makes 10

Heat the butter, sugar and golden syrup together in a small pan until the butter has melted and the sugar dissolved, stirring every now and then. Pour into a mixing bowl. Sift in the flour, cocoa and salt, mix thoroughly and leave to cool for 15 minutes.

Preheat the oven to 160°C (325°F) Gas 3.

Drop 10 teaspoonfuls of the chocolate mixture onto the prepared baking tray. Leave about 6–7 cm between them to allow the snaps to spread as they bake. Flatten them very slightly with the back of the teaspoon before baking in the preheated oven for 8 minutes. Leave to cool on the baking tray for 3–4 minutes before transferring to a wire rack to cool completely and become crisp – this will take only a matter of minutes.

Repeat with the second half of the mixture so that you end up with 20 rounds in total.

To make the filling, mix all the ingredients together in a bowl. Generously sandwich the snaps together with the filling. Lightly dust the top of each one with cocoa.

pear, mascarpone and orange tarts

Using ready-made and ready-rolled puff pastry makes life easy here. Slices of plum or dessert apple would also work well as a topping for these tarts.

300 g chilled ready-made, ready-rolled puff pastry

40 g butter

125 g mascarpone

3 tablespoons caster sugar, plus extra for sprinkling

finely grated zest of 1 small orange

75 g ground almonds

1 large egg yolk

4 ripe but firm small pears, cored and thinly sliced (no need to peel)

3–4 tablespoons smooth apricot jam

4 tablespoons toasted flaked almonds

2–3 large baking trays, lined with baking parchment and oiled

Makes 12

Preheat the oven to 220°C (425°F) Gas 7.

Take the pastry out of the fridge.

Melt the butter in a small pan and leave to cool slightly.

Put the mascarpone, sugar, orange zest, ground almonds and egg yolk in a bowl and mix. Refrigerate until needed.

Halve the pastry and roll one half out on a lightly floured work surface until it is about 2 mm – any thicker than that and the pastry won't crisp up in the oven. Trim the edges with a sharp knife to make a 21 x 24-cm piece, then cut that into six 7 x 12-cm rectangles. Arrange the rectangles on one of the prepared baking trays.

Repeat with the other half of the pastry.

Brush the edges of each rectangle with the melted butter and sprinkle a little sugar over them. Put 2 teaspoons of the mascarpone mixture in the centre of each rectangle. Spread the mixture out using a small knife, leaving a border of about 1 cm all the way round.

Top each tart with overlapping slices of pear and scatter a little more sugar over the top. Bake the tarts in the preheated oven for 15 minutes, or until the pastry is golden and crisp. Transfer to a wire rack.

Warm the apricot jam in a small pan, then use to brush over the pear slices. Sprinkle the flaked almonds over the top, then leave to cool.

fill the tins

courgette, carrot and pear cake with poppy seed frosting

200 g plain flour

100 g spelt flour

1 slightly rounded teaspoon baking powder

1 teaspoon bicarbonate of soda

1 tablespoon ground cinnamon

2 pinches of ground cloves

4 large eggs

275 g light muscovado or light brown soft sugar

250 ml virgin coconut oil or rapeseed oil

150 g carrots, grated (no need to peel)

100 g courgettes, grated (no need to peel)

2 medium pears, cored and chopped (no need to peel)

150 g walnut or pecan pieces

100 g sultanas

Poppy seed frosting

75 g unsalted butter, very soft

200 g cream cheese, chilled

100 g authentic Greek yoghurt, chilled

175 g icing sugar, sifted

1 tablespoon poppy seeds

two 20-cm sandwich tins, 4 cm deep, lightly buttered and base-lined with baking parchment

Serves 12

Coconut oil often solidifies in its container, so immerse the pot or jar in a bowl of hot water, from the kettle, for about 10 minutes to melt the oil. If you want to make this cake completely dairy-free, replace the butter, cream cheese and yoghurt in the frosting with 200 g soya cream cheese, sweetened with 2 tablespoons icing sugar. This cake will store well for a few days, but even longer if kept in an airtight container in the fridge. Serve it at room temperature.

Preheat the oven to 180°C (350°F) Gas 4.

Sift the flours, baking powder and bicarbonate of soda into the bowl of an electric mixer (or use a large mixing bowl and an electric whisk). Tip any spelt left in the sieve into the bowl too. Add the cinnamon, cloves, eggs, sugar and oil. Mix together.

In another bowl, mix the carrots, courgettes, pears, nuts and sultanas. Using a large metal spoon, fold these ingredients into the cake mix, making sure everything is thoroughly combined.

Divide the mixture between the prepared tins and spread it evenly with a spatula. Bake in the preheated oven for 40–45 minutes, or until risen, golden and set in the centre. Leave to cool in the tins.

To make the poppy seed frosting, whisk together the butter and cream cheese, add the yoghurt and icing sugar and whisk again – an electric whisk makes quick work of this. Stir in the poppy seeds, then refrigerate until needed.

Tip the cold cakes out of the tins and peel off the base papers. Place one cake on a board or serving plate, bottom-side uppermost. Spread half the frosting over it. Put the other cake on top, top-side uppermost, and spread the remaining frosting over the top.

tropical chai pineapple cake

200 ml boiling water

3 chai tea bags

350 g prepared fresh pineapple

250 g mixed soft dried tropical fruit, e.g. pineapple, papaya, mango, melon

100 g stoned, soft dates

150 g raisins

125 g dark muscovado or dark brown soft sugar

1 teaspoon bicarbonate of soda

1 tablespoon ground allspice

1 teaspoon freshly grated nutmeg

1 small cinnamon stick

3 star anise

4 tablespoons dark rum

150 g butter, chopped

grated zest of 2 limes

125 g plain flour

125 g self-raising flour

100 g shelled brazil nuts, chopped

2 large eggs, lightly beaten

3 tablespoons runny honey

dried pineapple slices, to decorate

a 20-cm round tin, 9 cm deep, lightly buttered and base-lined with baking parchment

Serves 16

This soft-textured, moist fruit cake keeps for up to two weeks and is flavoured with chai tea, which has warm undertones of cinnamon and ginger. If you can't find soft dried tropical fruit, use ready-to-eat dried apricots, pears, apples, peaches or prunes, or a mixture, instead.

Pour the boiling water into a measuring jug, add the tea bags, stir and leave aside while you prepare the rest of the ingredients.

Chop the pineapple into small pieces and set aside.

Chop the dried fruit and the dates into small chunks. Put into a medium pan with the raisins, sugar, bicarbonate of soda, all the spices, the rum and butter. Discard the tea bags from the chai tea and pour that into the pan too. Stir together and bring the mixture to simmering point over gentle heat.

When the butter has melted, increase the heat and boil the mixture for 2 minutes exactly, then transfer the contents to a large mixing bowl. Stir in the pineapple and lime zest and leave to cool completely, giving it a stir from time to time, as and when you remember.

Preheat the oven to 160°C (325°F) Gas 3.

Remove the cinnamon stick and star anise from the mixture. Sift both flours into the bowl and add the chopped nuts and beaten eggs. Stir well.

Tip the mixture into the prepared tin and spread it evenly with a spatula. Bake in the preheated oven for 1¾ hours, or until risen and deep golden brown. Leave to cool in the tin.

Tip the cold cake out of the tin and peel off the base paper. Warm the honey in a small pan, then use to brush all over the cake. Decorate with dried pineapple slices.

banana and passion-fruit loaf

For the best flavour, make sure your bananas are really ripe for this, even if they are at the stage when they have turned black in the fruit bowl and no one wants to eat them; they will be perfect to use in this loaf.

225 g self-raising flour

½ teaspoon bicarbonate
of soda

100 g butter, softened
and cubed

175 g caster sugar

2 large eggs, lightly beaten

3 passion fruit

3 very ripe bananas

To decorate

100 g icing sugar

1 passion fruit

dried banana slices,
to decorate

*a 19 x 9-cm loaf tin, 7 cm
deep, lightly buttered and
base-lined with baking
parchment*

Serves 8-10

Preheat the oven to 180°C (350°F) Gas 4.

Sift the flour and bicarbonate of soda into a bowl. Put the butter and sugar in an electric mixer (or use a large mixing bowl and an electric whisk) and beat until pale and fluffy. Add the beaten eggs and sifted flour mixture alternately to the bowl.

Halve the passion fruit and scoop out the pulp into a sieve over a bowl. Using a teaspoon, press and stir the pulp to extract the juice. Discard the leftover seeds. Peel and mash the bananas. Add the passion fruit pulp and mashed banana to the cake mixture and mix again.

Tip the mixture into the prepared loaf tin and spread it evenly with a spatula. Bake in the preheated oven for 55 minutes, or until golden and risen. Leave to cool in the tin.

To decorate, sift the icing sugar into a small bowl. Halve the passion fruit and scoop out the pulp into the bowl – no need to sieve the pulp this time. Mix together with a teaspoon. The icing sugar will seem stiff at first, but persevere until is thoroughly mixed. If the glaze still seems a little thick, add a drop or two of cold water – the consistency of the glaze will depend on the size of the passion fruit and how ripe it is. You want the glaze to be a thick, spreadable consistency.

Tip the cold loaf out of the tin and peel off the base paper. Spoon the glaze over the top of the loaf and decorate with dried banana slices. Leave to set for about 30 minutes before slicing.

sticky-topped treacle, marmalade and ginger loaf

This loaf keeps really well in a tin or airtight container for several days. It freezes well too, but add the marmalade topping after defrosting. This is a good one to slice and take on picnics or wintry walks.

125 g butter, softened and cubed

125 g dark muscovado or dark brown soft sugar

200 g plain flour, sifted

2 teaspoons baking powder

1 teaspoon ground ginger

2 large eggs, lightly beaten with 150 ml milk

4 tablespoons black treacle

5 tablespoons orange medium-cut marmalade

3 balls stem ginger in syrup, drained and finely chopped

100 g ready-to-eat dried apricots, snipped into small pieces

a 19 x 9-cm loaf tin, 7 cm deep, lightly buttered and base-lined with baking parchment

Serves 8-10

Preheat the oven to 190°C (375°F) Gas 5.

Put the butter and sugar in an electric mixer (or use a large mixing bowl and an electric whisk) and beat until combined. Tip in the flour, baking powder and ground ginger and add the egg mixture and black treacle. Mix everything together. Stir in 3 tablespoons of the marmalade, the chopped ginger and the apricots.

Tip the mixture into the prepared tin and bake in the preheated oven for 50 minutes. Leave to cool in the tin. Towards the end of cooling, gently heat the remaining marmalade and spread it over the top of the loaf. Leave to cool completely before carefully tipping the loaf out of the tin and peeling off the base paper.

apple and amaretto cake

This cake is quick to make and can be left to bake while you get on with other things. It freezes well and is delicious as is; for added indulgence, whipped cream mixed with a little icing sugar and almond-flavoured Amaretto makes a heavenly accompaniment.

450 g dessert apples

350 g plain flour, sifted

1 tablespoon baking powder

2 teaspoons ground cinnamon

200 g butter, softened and cubed

150 g light muscovado or light brown soft sugar

2 large eggs

100 ml milk

100 ml Amaretto

200 g sultanas

To decorate

3 small, red-skinned dessert apples

2 tablespoons runny honey

a 23-cm springform tin, 6 cm deep, lightly buttered and base-lined with baking parchment

Serves 8–10

Preheat the oven to 180°C (350°F) Gas 4.

Core, peel and chop the apples into 1-cm chunks.

Tip the flour, baking powder, cinnamon, butter, sugar, eggs, milk and Amaretto into the bowl of an electric mixer (or use a large mixing bowl and an electric whisk) and beat together until combined.

Using a large metal spoon, thoroughly stir in the chopped apples and the sultanas.

Spoon the mixture into the prepared tin and spread it evenly with a spatula.

To decorate, quarter the 3 red-skinned dessert apples. Don't peel them, but core them and thinly slice the quarters. Arrange the slices, slightly overlapping, on top of the cake in concentric circles.

Put the tin on a baking tray and bake in the preheated oven for 1½–1¾ hours, or until risen and golden and the apple slices on top are burnished. Cover the cake with foil towards the end of cooking to prevent over-browning, if necessary.

Warm the honey in a small pan, then use to brush over the top of the cake. Leave to cool in the tin before releasing it, peeling off the base paper and transferring to a plate or board to slice.

back-from-school traffic-light jam tarts

A goodie to have in the house for children when they return from school, starving, at teatime.

300 g ready-made shortcrust pastry

100–125 g each raspberry, apricot and greengage jam

a little beaten egg, for brushing (optional)

a plain or fluted 8–9-cm cookie cutter

a 12-hole shallow patty or bun tin, oiled

Makes 12

On a lightly floured work surface, roll out the pastry until it is about 2–3 mm thick. It may be easier to roll out half at a time. Using the cutter, stamp out 12 rounds and use to line the holes of the tin. Reserve the pastry trimmings. Chill the pastry-lined tin for 30 minutes.

Preheat the oven to 200°C (400°F) Gas 6.

Put about 2 teaspoonfuls of raspberry jam in 4 of the pastry cases, apricot jam in another 4 and greengage jam in the rest. Don't overfill them, otherwise the jam will bubble over the sides while they are cooking.

Re-roll the pastry trimmings and cut out short, thin strips of pastry. Place 2 parallel strips on top of each tart, twisting the strips as you do so and trimming them to fit the tarts. Press down the ends. Now place 2 more parallel strips at right angles to the first pair to create a lattice effect. Brush the lattice with a little beaten egg, if you like – it helps the pastry to brown.

Bake in the preheated oven for 20 minutes. Leave to cool for 5 minutes, then transfer to a rack to cool completely.

honey, toasted pine nut and pumpkin-seed flapjacks with chocolate topping

Vary the dried fruit you use in these flapjacks according to what you have handy. They are a hit with children and adults alike.

3 tablespoons pine nuts

2 tablespoons pumpkin seeds

175 g butter

100 g light brown soft sugar

3 tablespoons runny honey

100 g dried sour cherries or cranberries, or chopped ready-to-eat dried apricots, pears, peaches or prunes, or a mixture

250 g porridge oats

a pinch of salt

200 g milk chocolate, broken into pieces

a 20-cm square, loose-based tin, lightly buttered

Makes 24

Preheat the oven to 180°C (350°F) Gas 4.

Spread the pine nuts and pumpkin seeds on a baking tray and toast in the preheated oven for 5 minutes, or until lightly golden. Leave to cool, then roughly chop.

Gently heat the butter, sugar and honey together in a small pan until melted, stirring every now and then. Remove the pan from the heat and leave to cool slightly.

Tip the dried fruit and oats into a large mixing bowl. Add the salt and the chopped pine nuts and seeds. Pour in the warm butter mixture and mix well.

Tip the mixture into the prepared tin and press down firmly with the back of a spoon to make an even layer. Put the tin on a baking tray. Bake in the preheated oven for 30 minutes, or until lightly golden.

Meanwhile, melt the chocolate in a heatproof bowl set over a pan of barely simmering water. Pour over the flapjack, then leave to cool completely.

Remove the flapjack from the tin and cut into 24 bars.

really lemony gluten-free cake

The lemon zest and juice make this cake lovely and moist, and it will keep in an airtight tin for several days – store it whole and cut it as needed.

200 g butter, softened

200 g caster sugar

4 large eggs

150 g gluten-free self-raising white flour blend, sifted

2 teaspoons gluten-free baking powder

50 g polenta (cornmeal)

finely grated zest and juice of 1 lemon

Lemon syrup

75 g icing sugar

finely grated zest and freshly squeezed juice of 3 lemons

Candied lemons

250 g caster sugar

2 lemons

an 18-cm square tin, 6–7 cm deep, lightly buttered and base-lined with baking parchment

Serves 16

Preheat the oven to 180°C (350°F) Gas 4.

Put the butter, sugar, eggs, flour, baking powder, polenta and lemon zest and juice in an electric mixer (or use a large mixing bowl and an electric whisk) and beat until combined. Spoon the mixture into the prepared tin. Bake in the preheated oven for 45 minutes, or until risen, firm to the touch and golden.

Meanwhile, to make the lemon syrup, sift the icing sugar into a bowl and whisk in the lemon zest and juice with a balloon whisk. Set aside to allow the sugar to dissolve.

To make the candied lemons, put the sugar and 250 ml water into a pan. Gently heat, stirring, until the sugar has dissolved. Slice the lemons and flick out as many of the pips as you can. Add the lemon slices to the liquid in the pan – you want the lemons to cook more or less in a single layer. Bring to a simmer, then gently cook, uncovered, for 45 minutes, stirring from time to time.

When the cake is ready, take it out of the oven and make holes all over the surface with a fork. Spoon the lemon syrup over the cake, allowing it to seep in between spoonfuls – it will seem like a lot, but gluten-free flour is very absorbent. Leave the cake and candied lemons to cool completely.

Turn the cake out of the tin and arrange the candied lemons on top, discarding the liquid they were cooked in.

hazelnut, orange and marsala raisin biscotti

Biscotti are crunchy Italian double-baked biscuits and they will keep for a month or so, making them a great standby. Dip the biscotti into Vin Santo, limoncello, tea or a good espresso, as you eat them.

100 g raisins

2 tablespoons Marsala

250 g self-raising flour

25 g cocoa powder

1 teaspoon baking powder

150 g caster sugar

2 large eggs, lightly beaten

finely grated zest of
1 large orange

100 g blanched hazelnuts,
roughly chopped

*2 baking trays, lined with
baking parchment*

Makes about 30

Preheat the oven to 180°C (350°F) Gas 4.

Put the raisins in a small bowl with the Marsala, stir and leave to soak for at least 15 minutes.

Tip the flour, cocoa, baking powder and sugar into a food processor and whiz to mix. Add the beaten eggs and orange zest and whiz again for a couple of minutes until the mixture resembles coarse breadcrumbs. Tip the mixture into a mixing bowl and add the raisins and their liquid, and the chopped hazelnuts.

Using a spatula or wooden spoon, mix and knead everything together in the bowl until it starts to clump together – this will take a few minutes. Tip the dough out onto a lightly floured work surface and bring together into a ball with your hands.

Halve the dough and briefly knead each half. Roll each one into a 20-cm long log. Put both logs onto one of the prepared baking trays, leaving 8–10 cm between them to allow them to spread as they bake. Bake in the preheated oven for 35 minutes.

Remove the baked logs from the oven and leave to cool for 15 minutes, or until they are cool enough to handle. Meanwhile, reduce the oven temperature to 150°C (300°F) Gas 3.

Using a serrated bread knife, slice the logs on the diagonal into 1-cm thick slices. You should get about 15 slices from each log. Discard the ends.

Arrange the slices on the 2 baking trays in a single layer and bake them for a further 20 minutes to dry them out. Leave to cool on wire racks.

special
occasions

mulled wine and cranberry tea bread

This loaf is studded with juicy fruit and nuts, perfect for autumn and winter. It is delicious sliced and eaten as it is or spread with unsalted butter.

a wine-mulling spice bag

200 ml light, fruity red wine

1 tablespoon runny honey

75 g ready-to-eat dried figs

50 g crystallized stem ginger

75 g whole blanched almonds

50 g each dried cranberries and dried sour cherries (or use 100 g sultanas)

100 g light muscovado or light brown soft sugar

2 large eggs, lightly beaten

grated zest of 2 oranges

100 g fresh cranberries

225 g self-raising flour

1 teaspoon ground cinnamon

½ teaspoon ground allspice

Topping

75 g dried cranberries (or dried sour cherries, or sultanas)

2 tablespoons orange juice

4 tablespoons redcurrant jelly

a 19 x 9-cm loaf tin, 7 cm deep, lightly buttered and base-lined with baking parchment

Serves 12

First make the mulled wine. Put the wine-mulling spice bag in a medium pan with the red wine and honey. Slowly bring to a simmer, stirring now and then. Leave over very low heat for 5 minutes, then take the pan off the heat and set aside.

Roughly chop the figs, ginger and almonds and mix with the dried cranberries and cherries and the sugar in a mixing bowl. Remove the spice bag from the mulled wine, then pour the warm wine over the dried fruit and leave to soak for 30 minutes.

Preheat the oven to 160°C (325°F) Gas 3.

Stir the beaten eggs, orange zest and the fresh cranberries into the soaked dried fruit. Next, sift in the flour, cinnamon and allspice. Mix together until thoroughly combined.

Spoon the mixture into the prepared loaf tin. Bake in the preheated oven for 55 minutes, by which time the loaf will have risen and slightly shrunk from the sides of the tin. Leave to cool in the tin, then run a table knife around the edge of the tin, tip the loaf out and peel off the base paper.

To make the topping, gently heat the cranberries, orange juice and redcurrant jelly in a small pan over low heat, stirring until the jelly has dissolved.

Brush the top of the loaf with some of the sticky juices from the topping, then spoon the cranberries along the centre of the loaf. Leave to cool before serving.

snowman cookies

These are fun to make with children. If you don't want to have to buy three types of coloured icing, use red for both the noses and the mouths – or tiny pieces of candied peel also make fine snowman noses.

225 g self-raising flour, sifted

100 g butter, softened

100 g light brown soft sugar

1 large egg

1 tablespoon golden syrup

a pinch of ground cinnamon (optional)

To decorate

icing sugar, for dusting

400 g ready-to-roll white icing

2 teaspoons golden syrup

24 currants, halved

about 50 g ready-to-roll orange icing

about 50 g ready-to-roll red icing

150 g ready-to-roll black, blue or green icing

a plain 7-cm cookie cutter

2 baking trays, oiled

Makes 24

Put the flour, butter, sugar, egg, golden syrup and cinnamon, if using, in the bowl of an electric mixer and beat together until combined. Bring the dough together with your hands, then wrap in clingfilm and refrigerate for 1 hour or longer – even overnight is fine, if you want to get ahead.

Preheat the oven to 180°C (350°F) Gas 4.

Tip half the dough out onto a lightly floured work surface and roll out until it is 4–5 mm thick. Using the cutter, stamp out 12 rounds and arrange them on the baking trays. Bake in the preheated oven for 10–12 minutes, or until lightly golden. Leave to cool on wire racks.

Repeat with the other half of the dough.

To decorate, lightly dust the work surface and a rolling pin with icing sugar. Roll out half the white icing until it is 3 mm thick. Using the cutter again, stamp out 12 rounds. Repeat with the other half of the icing.

Put a dab of golden syrup in the centre of each cookie to act as glue and place a round of white icing on each one. Make 2 eyes on each snowman by pressing 2 currant halves into the icing quite firmly.

Next, using your hands, roll 24 small, carrot-shaped noses from the orange icing, making indentations along the length of each one with a small knife. Stick the noses onto the snowman faces with the tiniest dab of water.

Roll the red icing into 24 short, thin strips and pinch the ends. Stick one to each face for a mouth.

Using a rolling pin again, roll out the black, blue or green icing, in batches, and cut out hat shapes. Make indentations for the brims. Stick the hats on, then leave the snowmen to dry for an hour or so before serving.

ultimate chocolate fudge cake with honeycomb

This cake has a light, not-too-rich sponge and is perfect for a birthday cake – just add candles. If you want to get ahead, you can freeze the filled and topped cake, then defrost and sprinkle with the honeycomb to serve.

2 tablespoons cocoa powder

3 tablespoons boiling water

225 g self-raising flour

2 teaspoons baking powder

200 g butter, softened

250 g light muscovado or light brown soft sugar

2 tablespoons crème fraîche

1 teaspoon vanilla extract

4 large eggs, lightly beaten

Honeycomb

75 g caster sugar

2 tablespoons golden syrup

1 tablespoon bicarbonate of soda

Chocolate fudge icing

200 g dark chocolate (about 50% cocoa solids), broken into pieces

175 g crème fraîche

1 tablespoon vegetable oil

two 20-cm sandwich tins, 4 cm deep, lightly buttered and base-lined with baking parchment

a baking tray, lined with baking parchment

Serves 8

Preheat the oven to 180°C (350°F) Gas 4.

Dissolve the cocoa in the boiling water, then leave to cool. Sift the flour and baking powder into a bowl.

Put the butter and sugar in an electric mixer (or use a large mixing bowl and an electric whisk) and beat for 3–4 minutes, or until smooth and fluffy. Mix in the crème fraîche, vanilla extract and the cooled, dissolved cocoa. With the mixer running on a slow speed, add the beaten eggs and sifted flour mixture alternately to the bowl.

Divide the mixture between the prepared tins and spread it evenly with a spatula. Bake in the preheated oven for 25–30 minutes, or until firm to the touch. Leave to cool in the tins for 30 minutes. Tip out onto a wire rack and peel off the base papers. Leave to cool completely.

To make the honeycomb, put the sugar and golden syrup in a medium pan over gentle heat. Heat, stirring, until the sugar has melted. Increase the heat and bubble for 1 minute exactly. Take the pan off the heat and quickly stir in the bicarbonate of soda – the mixture will turn white and frothy. Immediately pour it onto the prepared baking tray and leave to cool until set.

To make the chocolate fudge icing, put all the ingredients in a heatproof bowl over a pan of barely simmering water and leave until smooth and glossy, stirring now and then. Take the bowl off the pan and leave to cool.

To assemble, place one cake on a board or large serving plate and spread about a third of the chocolate fudge icing over the top. Place the other cake on top and coat entirely in the rest of the icing. Chop the honeycomb into small chunks and sprinkle on top of the cake – any leftovers are a cook's perk!

rosewater, pistachio and grapefruit cake

You can buy crystallized pink rose petals in jars, or, to make your own, dip unsprayed petals in lightly beaten egg white followed by granulated sugar. Shake off the excess sugar, then leave the petals to dry on baking parchment until crisp. Serve the cake with Greek yoghurt sweetened with a little honey.

200 g shelled, unsalted pistachios

200 g self-raising flour

1 tablespoon bicarbonate of soda

150 g butter, softened and cubed

150 g caster sugar

3 large eggs, lightly beaten

2 tablespoons rosewater

4 tablespoons buttermilk

grated zest of 2 pink or red grapefruit

a few crystallized rose petals, to decorate

Grapefruit syrup

1 pink or red grapefruit

1 tablespoon rosewater

75 g caster sugar

a 23-cm springform tin, 6 cm deep, lightly buttered

Serves 10-12

Preheat the oven to 180°C (350°F) Gas 4.

Begin by whizzing 150 g of the pistachios in a food processor until finely ground. Roughly chop the remaining 50 g and mix three-quarters of them with the ground pistachios. Reserve the rest for scattering on the cake to decorate.

Sift the flour and bicarbonate of soda into the bowl of an electric mixer. Add the butter and mix together, on the lowest speed, until the mixture resembles clumpy breadcrumbs. Add the pistachios, sugar, beaten eggs, rosewater, buttermilk and grapefruit zest and mix until combined. The mixture will be thick, so you will probably need to stop a couple of times to scrape the mixture off the paddle.

Tip the mixture into prepared tin and spread it evenly with a spatula. Bake in the preheated oven for about 45 minutes, or until golden and risen.

Towards the end of the cooking time, make the grapefruit syrup. Squeeze the juice of the grapefruit through a sieve and into a medium pan. Add the rosewater and sugar to the pan and gently heat together, stirring, until the sugar has dissolved. Increase the heat and boil for 2 minutes to make the liquid slightly more syrupy.

When the cake is ready, remove it from the oven and, using a small, fine skewer, make a few holes over the surface of the cake. Spoon over the warm grapefruit syrup, allowing it to seep in between spoonfuls. Leave the cake to cool completely in its tin.

Once cold, pop the cake out of the tin and scatter the reserved chopped pistachios and a few crystallized rose petals on top.

victoria sandwich with fresh mint and strawberries

The sponges for this classic cake are best eaten as fresh as possible. They are also delicious sandwiched together with good-quality raspberry jam or a citrus curd and some whipped cream.

200 g unsalted butter, softened

200 g caster sugar

4 large eggs, lightly beaten

1 teaspoon vanilla extract

200 g self-raising flour, sifted

2 teaspoons baking powder

a pinch of salt

icing sugar, for dusting

Filling

250 g ripe strawberries

2 tablespoons icing sugar

grated zest of 1 unwaxed lemon

150 g crème fraîche, chilled

100 g mascarpone, chilled

1 tablespoon shredded mint leaves

two 20-cm sandwich tins, 4 cm deep, lightly buttered and base-lined with baking parchment

Serves 8

Preheat the oven to 180°C (350°F) Gas 4.

Put the butter and sugar in an electric mixer (or use a large mixing bowl and an electric whisk) and beat for 3–4 minutes, or until pale and fluffy. Gradually add the beaten eggs with the beaters still running, followed by the vanilla extract, flour, baking powder and salt. Mix until all the ingredients are combined.

Divide the mixture between the prepared tins and spread it evenly with a spatula. Bake in the preheated oven for 25 minutes, or until lightly golden and risen. Leave to cool in the tins for 30 minutes. Tip the cakes out onto a wire rack and peel off the base papers. Leave to cool completely.

To make the filling, hull and thinly slice the strawberries, then mix in a bowl with half the icing sugar and all the lemon zest. Leave to macerate for up to 30 minutes.

In another bowl, use a balloon whisk to whisk the crème fraîche and mascarpone together until smooth. Stir in the rest of the icing sugar and the shredded mint.

To assemble, place one cake on a board or large serving plate and spread the creamy filling over the top. Scatter the strawberries over the filling. Place the other cake on top and dust with icing sugar.

white chocolate and apricot roulade

This summer stunner, once assembled, will hold for a couple of hours before serving – keep it in a cool place, but not the fridge. To make it look extra special, use a vegetable peeler to make curls from a block of white chocolate to scatter on top.

4 large eggs

100 g caster sugar

2 pinches of saffron threads

100 g self-raising flour, sifted

3 tablespoons flaked almonds

1 tablespoon icing sugar, plus extra for dusting

Apricot filling

seeds from 4 cardamom pods, crushed

1 tablespoon orange blossom honey or other runny honey

1 tablespoon freshly squeezed lemon juice

8 apricots, stoned and finely chopped

White chocolate cream

75 g white chocolate, broken into pieces, plus extra if making curls

175 g crème fraîche

200 ml double cream

a 24 x 37-cm Swiss roll tin, 2.5 cm deep, oiled and base-lined with baking parchment

Serves 10-12

Preheat the oven to 190°C (375°F) Gas 5.

Break the eggs into a large heatproof mixing bowl and add the sugar and saffron. Place over a pan of simmering water, making sure the base doesn't touch the water. Using an electric whisk, whisk the ingredients for 5 minutes, or until pale and voluminous. Take the bowl off the heat. Using a large metal spoon, carefully fold the flour into the mixture.

Tip the mixture into the prepared tin and gently spread it evenly with a spatula. Sprinkle the flaked almonds over the top. Bake in the preheated oven for 12–15 minutes, or until lightly golden. Meanwhile, cover a large board with a sheet of baking parchment and sift the tablespoon of icing sugar evenly over it.

When the sponge is ready, leave it to settle, out of the oven, for 10 minutes. Run a small, sharp knife around the edges before turning it upside down over the sugared parchment. Remove the tin and peel off the base paper. Roll up the sponge from one of the shorter ends, rolling the sugared parchment with it as you do so – you may need to make a cut along the width of the sponge a couple of centimeters in, to help you start rolling. Leave to cool completely.

To make the apricot filling, put all the ingredients in a pan and simmer gently, uncovered, for 10 minutes – you want the apricots to be soft, but still retaining their shape. Leave to cool, then refrigerate until needed.

To make the white chocolate cream, put the chocolate and 2 tablespoons of the crème fraîche in a small heatproof bowl over a pan of barely simmering water. Leave until melted, stirring from time to time. Take the bowl off the heat and leave to cool slightly. Whisk the cream in a bowl until it forms soft peaks, then stir in the remaining crème fraîche and the cooled chocolate mixture.

Unroll the sponge onto a large board. Spread the white chocolate cream over it and scatter the apricot mixture on top. Roll up the roulade and dust with icing sugar.

cinnamon blueberry cake

Make this cake on the day you are going to eat it, but let it cool completely before assembling and serving.

175 g unsalted butter, softened

175 g caster sugar

4 large eggs, lightly beaten

a pinch of ground cinnamon

175 g self-raising flour, sifted

2 teaspoons baking powder

a pinch of salt

225 g blueberries

Cinnamon icing

200 g cream cheese, chilled

100 g crème fraîche, chilled

50 g unsalted butter, softened and cubed

150 g icing sugar, sifted, plus a little extra for dusting

2 teaspoons ground cinnamon

two 20-cm sandwich tins, 4 cm deep, lightly buttered and base-lined with baking parchment

Serves 8

Preheat the oven to 180°C (350°F) Gas 4.

Put the butter and sugar in an electric mixer (or use a large mixing bowl and an electric whisk) and beat for 3–4 minutes, or until pale and fluffy. Gradually add the beaten eggs with the beaters still running, followed by the cinnamon, flour, baking powder and salt. Mix until all the ingredients are combined.

Divide the mixture between the prepared tins and spread it evenly with a spatula. Bake in the preheated oven for 20–25 minutes, or until lightly golden and risen. Leave to cool in the tins for 30 minutes. Tip the cakes out onto a wire rack and peel off the base papers. Leave to cool completely.

To make the cinnamon icing, whisk all the ingredients together to combine.

To assemble, place one cake on a cake stand or large serving plate and spread two-thirds of the cinnamon icing over the top – a spatula or table knife is the ideal tool to use here. Scatter three-quarters of the blueberries on top of the icing.

Place the other cake on the blueberries and spread the remaining icing over the top. Finish with the rest of the blueberries. Dust with a little icing sugar.

chocolate chestnut brownie torte

This torte has the texture of a brownie, but it is as light as a feather. It doesn't contain any flour, which is an added bonus for anyone with an intolerance to wheat. In addition to being dusted with cocoa, it also looks pretty scattered with chopped *marrons glacés* – candied chestnuts.

200 g dark chocolate
(70% cocoa solids),
broken into pieces

175 g unsalted butter, cubed

5 large eggs, separated

175 g caster sugar

a pinch of salt

100 g tinned unsweetened
chestnut purée

cocoa powder, for dusting

a few chopped, toasted
hazelnuts, to decorate

*a 23-cm springform tin,
6 cm deep, oiled and base-
lined with baking
parchment*

Serves 8

Preheat the oven to 180°C (350°F) Gas 4.

Put the chocolate and butter in a heatproof bowl set over a pan of barely simmering water. Stir until the chocolate has melted and the mixture is smooth and glossy. Take the bowl off the heat and leave to cool slightly.

Put the egg yolks, 100 g of the sugar and the salt in the bowl of an electric mixer (or use a large mixing bowl and an electric whisk) and beat until pale and mousse-like – about 5 minutes. Mash and stir the chestnut purée with the back of a spoon in a small bowl, to break it up a bit, then whisk it into the egg-yolk mixture.

In a large, scrupulously clean bowl and using clean beaters, whisk the egg whites until they form stiff peaks. Add the remaining sugar to the egg whites, a quarter at a time, whisking after each addition.

Using a large metal spoon, carefully fold the melted chocolate mixture into the egg-yolk mixture. Finally, fold in the beaten egg whites. Be as gentle as you can so that you keep as much air in the mixture as possible.

Pour the mixture into the prepared tin and bake in the preheated oven for 40–45 minutes, or until well risen. Leave to cool in the tin. It will sink in the middle as it does so, but this is normal.

Transfer the tin to a large serving plate or board and release the side clip. Lift the ring from the torte and carefully slide the cake off the tin base, using a spatula or fish slice. Peel off the base paper. Dust the torte lightly with cocoa powder and scatter the chopped hazelnuts over the top.

apple, rum and raisin cupcakes

These are cupcakes with a difference – they contain all the flavours of a Caribbean rum punch: dark rum, spices and fruit.

100 g raisins

2 tablespoons dark rum

150 g butter, softened and cubed

150 g light muscovado or light brown soft sugar

2 large eggs, lightly beaten

175 g self-raising flour, sifted

generous fresh grating of nutmeg

2 dessert apples

1 ripe banana

finely grated zest of 1 orange

Icing

75 g icing sugar

½ teaspoon freshly grated nutmeg, plus extra for sprinkling

1 teaspoon dark rum

3–4 teaspoons freshly squeezed orange juice

a 12-hole muffin tin, lined with paper cupcake cases

Makes 12

Preheat the oven to 180°C (350°F) Gas 4.

Tip the raisins into a small bowl with the rum, stir and set aside while you make the rest of the mixture.

Put the butter, sugar, beaten eggs, flour and grated nutmeg in an electric mixer (or use a large mixing bowl and an electric whisk). Whisk together to combine.

Core, peel and chop the apples into small pieces. Peel and chop the banana into small pieces too and stir into the cake mixture with the apples, three-quarters of the orange zest and all the soaked raisins and rum.

Divide the mixture between the cupcake cases. Bake in the preheated oven for 25–30 minutes, or until risen and golden. Leave to cool on a wire rack.

When you are ready to ice the cupcakes, sift the icing sugar into a small bowl and stir in the grated nutmeg. Add the rum, then the orange juice, a teaspoon at a time, stirring between each addition – you may not need it all. Spoon the icing over the cupakes and sprinkle a little extra nutmeg and the remaining grated orange zest over each one. Leave to set before serving.

brown sugar pavlova with cinnamon cream and pomegranate

This is a perfect winter party piece. In the summer, top the meringue with summer berries or a mixture of sliced peaches or nectarines and blueberries instead.

4 large egg whites

50 g light muscovado sugar

175 g caster sugar
(unrefined is best here)

1 teaspoon cornflour

1 teaspoon white wine
vinegar

300 ml double or whipping
cream

1 tablespoon icing sugar

1½ teaspoons ground
cinnamon

125–150 g pomegranate
seeds

*a baking tray, lined with
baking parchment (don't
grease it, or your egg whites
will collapse!)*

Serves 8

Preheat the oven to 140°C (275°F) Gas 1.

Put the egg whites in a large, scrupulously clean bowl and whisk with an electric whisk (or use an electric mixer) until they form stiff peaks. Add the sugars, a tablespoon at a time, whisking constantly. Add the cornflour and vinegar with the final addition of sugar.

Pile the meringue mixture onto the prepared baking tray and form into a circle about 22 cm in diameter. Make swirls in the meringue with a skewer or the end of a teaspoon. Bake in the preheated oven for 1 hour, then turn the oven off and leave the pavlova in until cold – overnight is ideal.

To finish, whip the cream with the icing sugar and cinnamon to soft peaks. Pile it onto the pavlova and scatter the pomegranate seeds over the top.

index

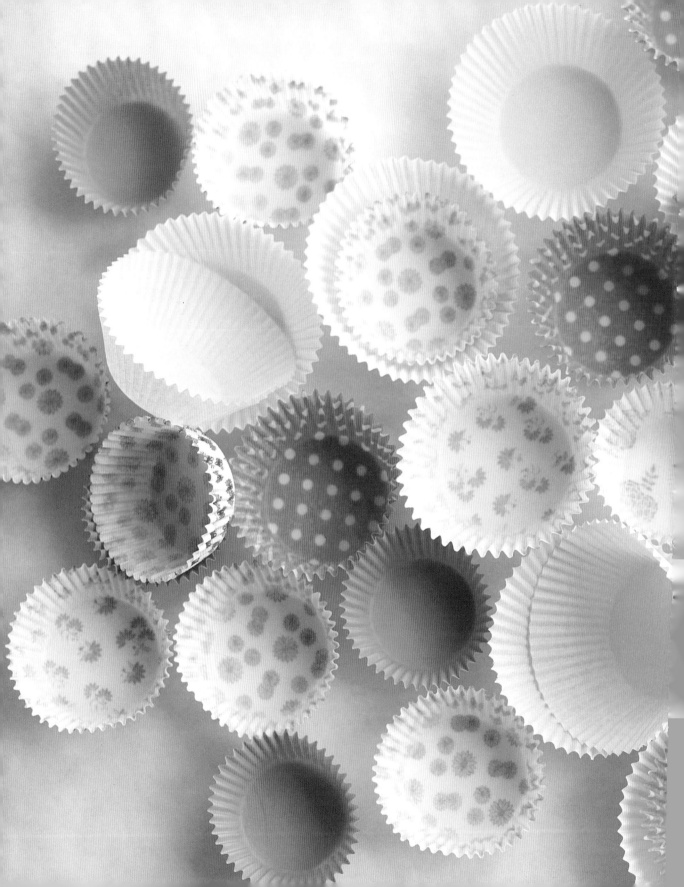